SO-AVC-161

From
Grandma
with
Love

A LEGACY OF VALUES

A collection of character-building stories
from real grandmothers

EDITED BY TONI THOMAS

A L
T I
PUBLISHING

ACKNOWLEDGMENTS

We would like to thank the following for their wonderful efforts in the creation of this book: Susan W. Hilbig, Sandra O'Rourke, Sherri Schottlaender, Rubén DeAnda, Claire, Evan, Guinevere & Norman Thomas, Rene Gandola, Betty Springer, Robert Erdmann, Victoria Light, Vicky White and the many grandmothers across the United States who submitted stories, including those whose contributions were not included in this volume.

Copyright © 1997 ALTI Publishing. All rights reserved. No part of this book may be reproduced in any form or by any electronic or mechanical means, including information storage and retrieval systems, without permission in writing from the publisher, except for a reviewer who may quote brief passages in review.

"Barnstormer's Daughter" is an adaptation from the previously published book, *Barnstormer's Daughter,* an autobiography by Norma L. Jones, copyright 1988. Used by permission of the estate of Norma L. Jones.

"The Carpenter" is copyrighted by Jon Murray 1996.

ISBN 1-883051-13-4
Library of Congress Catalog Card Number 96-86412

ALTI Publishing
Wayne B. Hilbig, President
P.O. Box 28025
San Diego, California 92198-0025 U.S.A.
(619) 485-1616

Ilustrations: Rubén De Anda
Copyediting: Sherri Schottlaender
Design: White Light Publishing

Printed in the United States of America

We do not have the answers to all your questions, but we can offer you a safe place when problems do happen. We offer you a place of rest from all the turbulence going on around you.

You are the generation of the future. We want to instill a return to values taken away by trends in society. We want to offer you a stable life.

When you were born, you became a light in our hearts; please do not let its glow grow dim. Remember, too, we love you no matter what or where you are or where we are. And wherever you are, we hope one day you read this and remember you are loved.

Josephine M. D'Antonio
Cherry Hill, New Jersey

President
GRANDPARENTS COUNT

About the Editor

Toni Thomas has been writing and editing for 20 years. Her works include songs, poems, stories and several plays. In addition to editing *From Grandma with Love*, she is also writing a musical about pioneer life in America. She lives in San Diego, California with her husband and three children.

CONTENTS

A lesson on ...

A lesson on ...

A lesson on ...

A lesson on ...

A lesson on ...

PREFACE

By some wonderful design, parents evolve into wise grand-parents. Perceptions of children tend to alter once the status of grandparent is achieved. So does one's view of the world.

A lifetime of rich experiences produces the quiet confidence needed to steady youth. However, today's children do not see as much of their grandparents as we did ours. Consequently, they are losing that subtle tutoring about life that has served society so well in the past.

Generations are often separated, but whether living in the same community or across the continent, most grandparents wish to reach out to help their children and grandchildren. They desire to leave a legacy of influence for good, a legacy of values.

The stories in **FROM GRANDMA WITH LOVE,** were selected from submissions by grandmothers across the nation. They are real-life experiences which, to the writers, became guideposts for living.

It is hoped that this book will help young people appreciate and more fully live the values which shaped the lives of their grandmothers. These experiences have the power to build character in all those who read them.

You too, whether young or old, will enjoy these stories. Some will pull at your heartstrings; some will make you laugh; others will remind you of your life. But all will influence you as you read this legacy of lessons learned and taught by wise, loving grandmothers. Experience is a great teacher.

Wayne B. Hilbig
Publisher

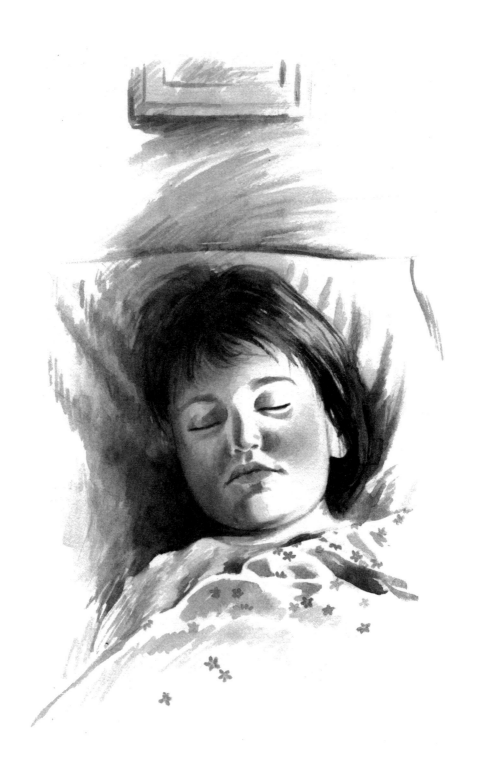

No More Monsters

When my granddaughter Rachael was about two and a half years old, she began having nightmares about monsters and other "scary things." She would wake up, screaming and crying for her mother in the middle of the night. Her mother would hold her trembling daughter and try to help her go back to sleep. But despite their efforts to reassure her, the nightmares continued. One day, exhausted, my daughter called me to see if I had any suggestions.

"Try hanging a picture of Jesus on the wall at the head of the bed," I recommended. "Tell Rachael that Jesus would never let monsters get into her bedroom." They decided to try my idea, so Rachael and her mother searched the house for a picture of Jesus; the problem was, they couldn't seem to find one.

"That's okay," suggested little Rachael. "Let's just hang up a picture of Grandmama. I know Grandmama wouldn't let monsters get me either." So the picture was hung in her room. And it worked: the monsters and the nightmares never returned.

— *Anonymous*

Ammon's First Words

From the beginning, Ammon's life took a different path. Born very prematurely, he weighed less than two pounds and he had to struggle to survive. When he finally came home from the hospital, he grew slowly but normally. Yet he never uttered a word. As time went on, we realized that his dealings with his brothers and sisters were always one-sided. Ammon never turned to them, never even seemed to notice that they were part of his world.

In time, Ammon was diagnosed as having autism, but we learned to carry on. Autism is a mental disorder that lessens a person's ability to communicate. Autistic people seem to be alone in a dream world all of the time. As the children in the family became old enough, we taught them how to help Ammon. Love was freely given, service rendered, and injuries forgiven. We included him as much as possible in the busy happenings of a large family.

"What is Ammon thinking?" Many times over the years we would wonder. The doctors could not give us any real insights into his mind. Ammon was our puzzle—could he even have thoughts and ideas that we would consider normal? We constantly tried to bring Ammon out of his silent, solitary world. Gradually, we could see that he was becoming more aware of people and things going on around him. He began to look at us when we talked to him. Still, he could not speak.

When Ammon was sixteen, I learned of a new way to communicate with autistic children that was having some success. It involved the therapist holding up the child's arm while he typed, which seemed to help him produce the actual typing motion. I decided to try this method with Ammon, and I made an appointment to visit Jerilyn, a therapist in this field.

I stood behind Ammon as Jerilyn worked with him. After awhile, she began to get some simple responses from him. Soon his typing became better, and across the screen came his first real words:

"Tell my mother I love her. Tell my mother I love her."

It was as if I had received a message from heaven, for I had never expected to hear those words from Ammon in this life. The words on the screen blurred as I realized that Ammon's joy at finally expressing his feelings must be as great as mine at being able to hear, at long last, from my silent son.

Erin Christensen ⏤ *San Diego, California*

Here Comes Santa Claus

"Ssssssshhhhh! Here he comes!"

I waited, holding my breath. Why was Santa taking so long? I was sure Grandpa had made a mistake this time, and was about to say so, when Santa Claus walked right into the room. There he was, red suit, shiny boots, and a big bag full of surprises. Santa paused, looked around the room, and listened for a moment to make sure everyone was sleeping. We all shivered in our places because we knew that if he found us, he would leave and not come back.

It's very important to have a good hiding place for Santa-watching, so we always practiced on Christmas Eve to make sure everybody knew what to do. With fourteen children, Mom, Dad, and who knows who might be joining us for Christmas that year, we had to be creative in finding hiding places. Some of the braver little ones crouched in the fireplace—of course, we cleaned it very well, just in case Santa decided to use it. We also set out milk and cookies where he'd be sure to find them, then off to bed we went to somehow try to sleep. Grandpa, who is a very light sleeper, would listen for Santa's sleigh, then sound the alarm: "I think I heard him! Quick, hide!"

Now that Santa was satisfied that not a creature was stirring, he opened his sack and began going through his list.

"Let's see . . . Jamie. He's done really well this year getting along with his sisters," said Santa, as he set a package under the tree. He continued through the family, naming each of us by name. Halfway through our family's long list, Santa sat down and rested, munching a cookie and drinking the glass of milk we had provided. We thought he'd never finish!

After all the presents were out of the bag and under the tree, Santa walked over and looked up the chimney.

"Shall I go up the chimney this time?" Santa muttered to himself. "No. I'm getting too old for that," he decided, much to the relief of the two terrified children hiding in the dark corners of the fireplace. Instead, it was "Merry Christmas," and off he went, out the back door. When we heard the door close, we ran to open our gifts, with squeals of delight and merry pleasure.

Unfortunately, that year two of the children were not happy with their presents. They had asked for something that Santa didn't think they were old enough to have, so he wisely brought them something else. In their disappointment, they grumbled and forgot to be grateful. They did their best to make everyone else miserable, too.

Finally the day ended and we all went to bed, but to everyone's surprise, when the two ungrateful children awakened the next morning, their toys were gone! In the middle of the night, Santa's elves had returned and taken back the presents. The toys were never seen again.

Christmas is a time for giving, but in our family we always felt that it's important to not go overboard. We never get everything we want in life, but we need to appreciate what we do have. Our family will never forget that Christmas; now every year when the children write letters to Santa, they ask for what they'd like to get, but they always include: "We'll be happy with whatever you bring us."

— *Anonymous*

A lesson on gratitude...

Susan

After raising five children, being blessed with eleven grandchildren, and teaching elementary school for umpteen years, I have had many opportunities to learn what is really important in life. But no one has taught me a more poignant lesson than Susan.

Susan's family was what some cruelly called "poor white trash." Neither parent worked, and the family lived entirely on welfare. Lacking many of the luxuries of life, the children often came to school in dirty, ragged clothes. The other students made fun of them unmercifully.

When Susan came through my class, I was teaching remedial reading and only saw her for forty-five minutes each day. Nevertheless, as Christmas approached, nine-year-old Susan announced that she wanted to buy me a Christmas gift. Her mother had told her they couldn't afford one, but Susan was hopeful that somehow there would be a way.

"Susan, you're a good artist," I said. "What if I give you paper and markers and you draw a picture for me to frame and hang in my classroom?" Susan didn't like that idea at all. She wanted to get me something "nice."

Three days before Christmas break, Susan still hadn't been able to buy me a gift. I reassured her that it wasn't necessary. She tearfully informed me that she also couldn't come to school the last day before Christmas vacation. Her family couldn't afford to buy a present for the customary class gift exchange.

However, much to my surprise, Susan entered my room at 7:20 a.m. that last day of school. Her face glowed as she approached me with her hands behind her back.

"Susan! How nice to see you," I said, smiling at her. "I thought you weren't coming today."

"I'm not," she explained. "My mother's waiting in the car to take me back home, but she brought me to school early so I could give you your present."

The gift she held out to me was wrapped in the colored Sunday comics pages. It was flat and I thought at first she had drawn a picture for me after all.

"I hope you like it!" she said as I took the present from her. "I've begged Mama for three weeks to let me have it. It was the nicest thing we had in our house."

Tears filled my eyes as I looked at her gift. It was a picture of a hunting dog. It had been taken from the top of a calendar and had holes in all four corners where it had been tacked to the wall. But it was beautiful to me; that was the only time in my life that someone had given me "the nicest thing" they owned.

I had made small bags of candy for each of my seventy students. As I gave Susan a hug and her candy, she excitedly said, "Oh, candy! I'll share this with my brothers and sister. Mama already said she couldn't afford to buy any this year, so it will probably be all we get." I had a strong urge to give her all the bags of candy I had made.

Shortly after Susan left to go home, the first group of students came to my classroom. As I wished them "Merry Christmas!" I handed a bag of candy to each one.

"Well, gawl," said Lee, looking at his candy. "Is this all you're giving us?"

All these years I have remembered the reaction of those two children: Susan had so little but gave the nicest thing she owned; she was excited and thankful for a small bag of candy. Lee gave nothing and appreciated nothing.

Since then, that picture of a dog has hung in my classroom. It reminds me of what is important in life. Each year as I tell my students the story of Susan, I hope it helps them know what is important, too.

Sharon Larkins — Danielsville, Georgia

Where Are You, Madia?

I missed you, Gramma," you used to say. "I miss you as soon as I leave here. The last time when I went out the door, I started missing you."

From the time you were almost six to when you were fourteen, I kept a list of your sayings. Some were cute:

"Gramma, what are the lines on your leg, the ones that look like thunder?"

Still others were profound:

"Look at the clouds moving, Gramma. Is God pushing them?"

You were a loving, bright, funny, thoughtful little girl, and I wrote your words down to be sure you and your children would know how you thought as a child. I always had a special relationship with you: we'd share thoughts and feelings, and I wanted to teach you important things, and show you the world.

"Don't grow up, Madia," I would tease. "Promise Gramma you won't grow up to be a teenager."

But you did. Now you are a stranger, with no place left for me in your life. It's a very empty feeling, as if someone had died.

I have a treasure chest of your childhood sayings according to Gramma. Occasionally I bring out some of the gems and go over them:

"Gramma, if I get another dollar, I'm going to buy you a bathing suit. Then you can go in the sprinkler with me. I am, really! What kind do you want — Mickey Mouse?"

"I know you're busy with Christmas, Gramma, but you gotta help me make this bell for my mother. Mothers are more important than Christmas. Food is important, too, but mothers are most important."

Do you remember any of these? Do you miss those times? I do. I miss you, Madia, and hope we will rediscover each other again. After all, that loving, thoughtful little girl is still someplace inside you. Where are you, Madia?

Shirley Silko ⏤ *Milwaukee, Wisconsin*

The Gift

*R*ings and jewels are not gifts but apologies for gifts. The only true gift is a portion of thyself," wrote Ralph Waldo Emerson. Often we show our love to others with a gift, but the best gifts require sacrifice. Ten years ago, my son had the opportunity to give his sister Jody a true gift, the gift of life.

In 1979, Jody gave birth to her fourth child, but after the baby was born, she never regained her strength. Her joints were red and hurting, and she was very weak. Finally Jody's problem was diagnosed as lupus, a life-threatening disease. In lupus, the immune system destroys major organs of the body. Although she was given very strong drugs, within a few years Jody's kidneys had failed and she had developed severe heart damage. The doctors told us that her only hope of survival was a kidney transplant.

When we heard the news, each member of our family volunteered to donate a kidney, but there were many things that had to be taken into consideration. In order for Jody's body to accept the kidney, the donor had to have similar blood and tissue types. We were all tested, but only my son David matched well enough.

David eagerly agreed to the gift, although I know it must have been a little scary for him. As a baby, he had had to have surgery on his feet, then had both legs in casts for a long time; afterwards, he had a terrible fear of doctors and hospitals. Nonetheless, David never faltered—he agreed to go ahead with the surgery.

The morning of the surgery, our family waited anxiously in the waiting room, praying that both Jody and Dave would be all right. I sensed, however, that something peculiar was going on.

"What is happening?" I asked a nurse who was moving David's hospital bed.

"There's a problem in surgery," he replied.

Well, in my panic and fear for my two children, I ran right into the operating room! The surgeons were surprised to see me there, but kindly explained the problem. During the surgery, Jody's heart had stopped and they had to stop the operation to revive her. The doctors had already started Dave's surgery, so they had to patch him up until Jody was well enough for the surgery.

When David came to, he was in a lot of pain. The doctors had made a twelve-inch cut across his abdomen, and had removed a rib in order to get to the kidney. Imagine waking up and being told that the surgery had not been finished, and that you'd have to do it again the next day!

Without hesitation, David went ahead with the second surgery, and the operation was an immediate success. Although it took Dave many long months to recover, Jody instantly improved, her color returning as the new kidney started working.

David truly gave his sister the gift of life. The doctors had given Jody three months to live before the surgery, but now, ten years later, she is still living. Donating a kidney was a real sacrifice for David and a true gift: he truly gave of himself.

Marietta Clark — *Bountiful, Utah*

A Boat of My Own

A punishment was never too high on my list of things to look forward to. As a child, I certainly didn't appreciate the value of the lessons I learned from those experiences. The punishment that I remember the most, however, makes me realize how very smart my dad was.

I grew up in a small Michigan town on the shores of Lake St. Clair. Since a network of canals connected our town to the lake, the most important moment in my young life would be the day I became old enough to have a boat of my very own. One beautiful sunny morning, I knew that that day was only a few weeks away. But for some reason, I just couldn't wait.

Dad's boat was docked in the boathouse with a full tank of gas.

"Let's go, I can drive it," my friend Mike said. "We won't hurt it; we'll only go for a little ride." That was all it took for me to forget temporarily all the rights and wrongs I'd been taught. I knew the boat was strictly off-limits, but the fun we would have seemed to far outweigh any consequences.

We got aboard and Mike jumped in the back of the boat so that he could drive. The boat wasn't large or expensive; it was just a fishing boat with an outboard motor, but to my Dad, it was a cabin cruiser. It didn't take long for Mike to start the motor, and we untied the mooring from the dock and pushed off.

Then the unbelievable happened! As Mike tried to get the motor in reverse, it jumped full-throttle into forward gear, flying dead-ahead into the dock. The sound of wood splintering and the motor revving was more than I could bear. Forcing my eyes open, I saw a huge, gaping hole in the side of the boat. The boat didn't sink, at least not as much as my heart. "Oh, no! What do we do now?"

My dad was not due home for four hours, four long, miserable hours of dreading the punishment to come. When he finally did get home, I was too afraid to tell him what had happened, so my little sister had to do the confessing. I can still remember the look of anger and disappointment on his face.

Then, a second unbelievable thing happened that day: without saying a word to us, Dad just turned and walked away. After more waiting, wondering, and dreading, we saw him come home with new ribs for the boat, along with scrapers, sandpaper, and paint. He put us to work repairing the boat. It took us awhile, but when we had finished, the boat looked almost as good as new. Then, lo and behold, he gave the boat to my sister and me. But you know, I never did enjoy being in that boat again.

He was awfully smart, that old dad of mine. For you see, every time we got into that boat, we punished ourselves much more than any punishment he could have meted out would have. Thanks, Dad!

Arlyne Sikon ⏤ Amarillo, Texas

Be Sure to Leave on Time

I was a teenager in 1944, living in Maison Laffitte, France, under the German Occupation. During World War II, the Germans had invaded my country, and soldiers with machine guns were patrolling the streets where I lived. England was just across the English Channel from us, and they were fighting the Germans too. At any hour, they might run a bombing raid against the German forces, trying to weaken the German army. When we heard the planes flying overhead, we escaped to the cellar. When there was no time to take cover, my mother would say, "Hide under the bedsheets and pray to God."

That summer I worked near the railroad station in a shop that sold silk stockings. My job was to mend the torn stockings that customers brought in. One particular day, it was almost time to stop and go home for lunch. I knew that my mother was expecting me at twelve o'clock, but I was tempted this once to stay as long as I could to finish my work. Every day at about one o'clock, the German authorities turned off the electricity in our city. If I went home at noon I would not be able to use the electrical mending machine when I returned; instead I would have to mend by hand, a very tedious task. I decided to stay.

As I continued working, drawing the silk threads together, I thought of my mother. Before I had left that morning, she had said, "Be sure to leave on time..." I knew she'd be worried when I didn't arrive as scheduled, so I changed my mind and gathered my things to go home.

I had just crossed a large bridge that spans the Seine River near my home when I heard bombers overhead. I frantically took cover until the planes had passed and all the bombs had dropped and detonated. One bomb struck the bridge I had just crossed. I hurried home.

When it was safe, my Mother and I went to see the damage done by the attack. I remember walking back across the damaged bridge upon some rickety boards, hastily placed over the holes the bomb had made. Between the boards I saw the river flowing swiftly below, and it frightened me. But the biggest shock was seeing the little stocking shop. The planes had targeted the nearby train station, and the stocking shop was destroyed along with it. Nothing remained of the building where I had been working only moments before the air raid.

War is a terrible thing, but I did learn a valuable lesson about obedience. That day, the difference between life and death was that I had listened to my mother's words: "Be sure to leave on time..."

Pat Bigler — Poway, California

Hobo Soup

I grew up during the Great Depression, and we were very poor. When I was just a girl, the stock market crashed and many businesses in our country failed. Without jobs, there was no money to buy food or other necessities. Despite our poverty, we found simple ways to entertain ourselves—we had grapevine swings, a swimming hole in the nearby creek, and a sweet bay tree that bent over close to the ground that we would run up and jump off of. It was a lot of fun. There was no money for flower seeds so we would go into the countryside and dig up wildflowers to transplant in our yard. We always had something to look forward to, a different plant in bloom.

But life was not always fun. When we ate Mama would tell us not to take the last bit from the serving bowl, for someone might come by who was hungry. A lot of people did come by, begging for food, work, or a place to sleep. Papa would talk to them, and if they seemed honest and worthy, he gave them shelter for a few days in exchange for work.

Mama kept all the food we left in our bowls at mealtimes and sealed it up in fruit jars. When Sunday came, she made a big pot of soup out of all the leftovers she had saved for the hoboes, which is what homeless people were called then. All our friends would come home with us from church to enjoy Mama's hobo soup.

Some people did not even have a roof over their heads. When we had extra vegetables on our farm, Papa took them to other people who were hungry. Once I went with him, and I saw people living in cardboard boxes, tar-paper shacks, or ragged tents. I saw one little boy who was sitting out naked in the cold weather, and I laughed at him. When Papa heard me laughing, he was offended, so he sent me to the truck to wait for him.

When we arrived home, I was sent to bed in a cold room with nothing to eat. After two hours, Papa came and took me to the warm kitchen for some hot food. After I had eaten, he took me on his knee and asked me if I had learned anything. I told him I had learned that it was not funny to be hungry and cold.

I have never forgotten that day and that lesson. I am fortunate now to be able to share with the less fortunate, and to help my fellow men as I see the need. I always want people to eat when they visit me because I have never forgotten Mama's hobo soup and the many people who would have gone hungry without it.

Bertie D. Conn ⚊ *Pineville, Louisiana*

Family Over Fame

I guess it's every girl's dream to be a glamorous movie star. I suppose I was lucky—it really happened to me. After I graduated from George Washington University, I decided to go to New York to study acting under Maria Oustensjaya at the American Theater. She was very famous at the time. One day, I was acting the part of Ophelia from Shakespeare's *Hamlet* when some talent scouts saw me. They offered me a screen-test, which I took, and they sent me to Hollywood.

In Hollywood, I worked for Metro-Goldwyn-Mayer for a year. It was really very interesting. I knew Clark Gable, Greta Garbo, and other famous stars of the day. I had the chance to use the wardrobe—I could wear any other movie star's clothes if I wanted to—and I did wear some beautiful clothes. But I didn't like the atmosphere on the set, so I took books with me, and while I waited I studied Russian literature, reading Dostoyevsky and Tolstoy.

Probably the biggest picture I made was *Tailor-Made Man*. Then after one year, they wanted me to sign up for another year. Depending on how I did in the next two or three movies—I had to prove I could be popular—I could break into something big. I did get a big offer with quite a bit of money, but I turned it down. I just wanted to marry my sweetheart, George.

George and I had met in high school. I was a sopho-more then, and he was a senior. He and two other boys came to pick up me and a friend for a picnic and we had a lot of fun. I had a ukulele, and I was playing and singing silly songs. Well, afterwards, George began asking me out and I was just delighted. It was very exciting. Can you imagine? He never took out anyone else but me after that. George was just a great guy and I knew that I wanted to marry him much more than I wanted to be in movies.

I have had the most wonderful life anyone could imag-ine. I had the most outstanding husband; we were married sixty-four years. I learned the only things that really matter in life are love and family. If we have wonderful relationships, we will have a wonderful life. It is not the glamour, not the out-side things—those do not last. I could have been there on top for awhile, but it would have passed; I would have gotten old. Beauty and age change but your relationships with the people you love last forever.

Lenore Romney ― *Bloomfield Hills, Michigan*

Lenore and George Romney have had distinguished careers. Lenore hosted radio programs in Washington, D.C., and Detroit, Michigan. She ran for the United States Senate as the Republican Party candidate in 1970. George was president of American Motors Corporation before being elected to three terms as governor of Michigan, and he served as Secretary of Housing and Urban Development in the cabinet of President Richard Nixon.

The Ruler

When I was a first-grader, I loved my teacher, Mrs. Young. She was tall and had very black hair. We went to school in a three-room schoolhouse with the first grade and the second grade in the same room. Every day when we had singing time, Mrs. Young asked me to lead the class.

One day, Mrs. Young gave each child a gift. It was a wooden ruler. She showed us the ruler and told us that twelve inches make one foot. Then she told us to turn the ruler over, for she had another lesson for us to learn that day. Mrs. Young taught us to read and say what was written on the back:

"Do unto others as you would have them do unto you."

Mrs. Young taught us what a good rule that was for all of us. We tried to remember and follow that Golden Rule. It worked for us then, and it will still work for you today.

Reverend Nancy White — Bluefield, West Virginia

No Horse of Mine

*M*y father grew up in a small Nevada farming community. Rainfall is scarce in Nevada, so farms are irrigated by a system of canals. Farmers have what are called water rights, that allow them to divert the flow of the canal water onto their fields on selected days for a certain amount of time. As a youth, it was my father's job to change the head gates when it was their turn to water their crops.

One day, Dad rode off on a horse to lower the gates, and when he returned through town, he passed the pool hall. A bunch of his friends were hanging around, and they called out to him.

"Come on in, Kenneth. Let's play a game of pool."

Well, Dad knew that a pool hall was not the kind of place he should be going to, and he knew that he had work to do at home, but he decided to stop for a while and play a game of pool with his pals.

While Dad was inside, his father had some errands to run, so he hitched up a horse and wagon and went on into town. When Grandfather went by the pool hall and saw the horse there, he said nothing to Kenneth, but he untied the horse, put it behind the wagon, and took it home.

When my father came out of the pool hall, he realized his horse was gone.

"Who stole my horse?" he asked a couple of oldtimers who were sitting there passing the time of day.

"Your Dad did," they responded.

Well, my dad was really angry and went stomping off. It was time to change the water again, and he knew he'd have to walk there and all the way back home. When he finally reached home, he confronted his father.

"Dad, what did you take that horse for?"

"Kenneth," Grandfather responded, "I can't force you to stay out of the pool hall, but no horse of mine is going to be tied to one."

That really made my dad think. If his father's horse was too good to be tethered in front of a pool hall, maybe he hadn't ought to be there either. That experience taught my dad an important lesson about honoring the family name. Though he had been taught better, and he knew he shouldn't go to a pool hall, by doing so he had made his whole family look bad.

A family's good name is important. We should always do our best to honor and protect our family name.

Alice Packard — *Carlsbad, California*

The Five Dollar Bill

I'm sorry, honey, but that five dollar bill isn't yours." I looked at my grandfather in shock! What did he mean that five dollar bill wasn't mine? I had worked hard for it.

My older sister and I were spending part of our summer with my grandparents on their farm in Missouri. Their neighbor, a few miles down the road, had huge fields of strawberries and needed pickers to harvest them. Granddad had offered to help, and I asked if I could go along. At ten years old, I was eager to make some money of my own. Since I would be in Granddad's care, my grandmother consented to let me go and give it a try.

Although we arrived early the next morning, several people were already there. Granddad introduced me to his neighbor, Mr. Goodnight, who was a large, jolly old fellow. Mr. Goodnight handed me a strawberry crate and cautioned me not to eat too many strawberries. Granddad explained to me how picking strawberries worked. The crate was a small wooden tray that held six quart-size strawberry boxes. After filling all six boxes with berries, you carried the tray back to Mr. Goodnight, who marked it down. At the end of the day, he paid you according to the number of boxes you had filled.

Working beside my grandfather, I eagerly filled baskets. I had never seen so many big, red, juicy strawberries. I couldn't resist trying one. Have you ever eaten a ripe strawberry, warm from the sun? Heavenly!

It didn't take long to realize that picking berries is hard on the back. I found it was easier to crawl along on my knees than to constantly bend over, and I could see the strawberries better as they hid beneath the vines. Though it was hard work, talking and joking with my grandfather made the work easier.

My proudest moment came at quitting time when Mr. Goodnight paid us. He gave me a five dollar bill for my labors. All the way back to Granddad's house, I turned the bill over and over, looking at it, just wanting to touch it. I couldn't keep the grin off my face and I couldn't wait to show it to Grandma. Then to my utter dismay, there in the kitchen, Granddad had announced that it wasn't mine!

"What do you mean, Granddad?" I asked. "I worked all day for this; why isn't it mine?"

Granddad pulled me over onto his lap. Stroking my long braids, he gently asked: "Didn't you borrow five dollars from your sister when you went shopping with Grandma the other day?"

Dumbfounded, I nodded yes. How had he found out about that? Granddad then taught me one of the greatest lessons of my life.

"If someone has a five dollar bill in their pocket," he stated, "but they owe someone five dollars, then that money isn't theirs." It was a lesson about debt that I have never forgotten.

I have to admit that it hurt to hand that five dollar bill to my sister, but to this day, forty years later, that principle has stuck with me. I have always paid my debts on time, and I pay them first before I count any money as my own. It's a debt of integrity that I will always owe my grandfather. Thanks, Granddad.

Pat Curtis — Yuma, Arizona

A lesson on brotherhood...

Jefferson

Christmas carols laced with children's laughter sifted through the cheerful halls of Milwaukee Children's Hospital. Outside, snow plastered the deep windows. It was Christmastime, but not a happy time for our youngest child. Two-year-old Betsy had leukemia.

Betsy was born with Down's Syndrome and was going to be a baby longer than most. She was slow to talk and walk, but quick to notice people, quick to love and be happy. She missed her brothers and sisters, and they missed her too.

Every afternoon, Betsy greeted me with smiles and big hugs when I rushed into her room at the hospital. Five-year-old Jefferson, who had the bed next to her crib, would say:

"Look, Betsy! Here's Mama!"

Betsy and Jefferson had become playmates, playing peek-a-boo with their covers. When she dropped her stuffed toys over the crib rail, he scampered over to pick them up for her. Betsy would laugh and say, "Ta ta," which meant "thank you."

That day when I came in, Betsy was napping. Jefferson put his finger to his lips to tell me. When she stirred and saw me sitting next to her, she opened her arms. I picked her up and kissed her soft blond hair.

"Mama, Mama," she said, stroking my face.

Her dinner was ready for her on a tray beside her bed. I sat her on my lap and started to feed her. She closed her lips tightly, however, and turned her head away from the spoon. Jefferson was sitting on his bed with the tray on his lap—he loved to eat in bed. "Nummy, Betsy. It is good!" he urged, attacking his food with smiles. Betsy shook her head and reached for the glass of juice.

"Thanks, Jefferson," I said. "Thanks for helping, but I better go talk to the nurse." When I put Betsy on my shoulder, her heat radiated through my clothes. Her arms hung limply and her eyes were half-closed. We walked slowly down the hall to the nurse's station. Jefferson slipped off of his bed and followed us. He reached for Betsy's dangling hand and held it gently. We were a procession!

"She is very warm," the nurse said. "I'll get the doctor on call. Could you take her back to her bed?"

"Of course." So we—Betsy, Jefferson, and I—returned to their pastel-colored room. Once again, we were a parade. Jefferson shuffled along in his slippers, keeping pace while clasping her hand.

I sat down with her in the rocking chair.

"Hi, Betsy. Look, here's your teddy bear," Jefferson coaxed. His eyes shone with love, tenderness, and concern. He stood next to us, still holding her hand, as I rocked and cradled her in my arms. With his free hand, he blew her a kiss.

"Love ya, Betsy." She opened her eyes and tried to smile.

When the doctor came, he transferred Betsy to a private room on another floor so she wouldn't catch any germs from the other patients.

We never saw Jefferson again. But the picture I'll carry forever is of her tiny pink hand, comforted and folded gently into a slightly larger, brown hand. Two children, one black and one handicapped—they knew everything of love and nothing of prejudice.

Mary Rosina Baer ⟶ *South Milwaukee, Wisconsin*

Oh, Help Me!

s a child, I learned to pray at my mother's knee. She taught me to always thank God, and to ask for His help to be good. "He is always there to help you when you pray," she promised. One summer, I learned that lesson for myself.

In July of 1963, my back was giving me a great deal of pain. Although I'd had back problems for years, this time the pain was the worst I'd ever felt. I decided to see a doctor who had been recommended by several friends. Unfortunately, when I called to make an appointment, I learned that he would be out of town for two weeks. I just couldn't go on without help, so I went to see a chiropractor.

Since I couldn't walk by myself, my son, Dea, took me to the chiropractor's office. The chiropractic treatment relieved much of the pain, and I made another appointment to see the doctor the following week. Meanwhile, he warned me not to lift anything, not even a pan of water from the stove. He showed me how to get in and out of cars and chairs, etc., in a way that wouldn't reinjure my back.

For the next week, I was very careful to follow the doctor's directions, and I got along quite well. Then one morning, as I was going in and out of the house, I noticed that my neighbor, Marion Kerby, was working underneath his son's car. As I was preparing lunch, I heard a crash and a yell. I knew right away what had happened — the car had fallen and crushed Mr. Kerby. I ran to the phone and called for help.

As I was calling, Marion's wife, Viva, rushed in to tell me what had happened. As soon as I hung up the phone, I went right over.

"What will I do?" Thoughts raced through my mind as I ran out the door. "Is there a pipe or a pole I can use for a lever? I'M NOT SUPPOSED TO LIFT ANYTHING! Not even a pan of water from the stove."

When I reached the scene, it was obvious there was only one thing to do — somehow we had to lift that car. As I took hold of the bumper, I whispered a prayer, "Oh, help me!"

Instantly, directions for lifting came clearly to my mind.

"Bend your knees, keep your back straight!"

We lifted together. It didn't seem like anything was happening, but we heard Marion call, "Quick, pull me out!"

Miraculously, I was able to hold up that car while Viva pulled him out. Luckily, Marion was on a crawler with wheels. I eased my hold on the bumper, and lowered the car. When the ambulance arrived, Marion was rushed to the hospital, where they discovered that he had seven broken ribs, a punctured lung, and a concussion to his heart. If he'd been pinned under the car any longer, he would have died. Although it took Marion a while to mend, he eventually regained good health.

As news of the incident spread, Viva and I became quite famous in our town. My brother-in-law, who was in charge of the local Fourth of July celebration, jokingly asked me if I'd perform at the carnival — "Come see the lady lift the car!"

It truly was a miracle that we lifted that car. For days afterward, I had ridges on my fingers where the bumper had rested, and my rings were so smashed that I had to have them cut off. I was just grateful that God had answered my prayer, and I am thankful that my mother taught me to pray when I needed help. We're never alone, you know. God is always there for us.

Maxine Montague — Mesa, Arizona

World War II in Wales

I was nine when World War II started in Britain, in 1939. My father was Secretary General for the YMCA, and our family was sent to live at an artillery camp at Rhyl in Northern Wales. He managed the YMCA that was there as recreation for the men.

In the early part of the war, the German planes often flew over Rhyl to get to Liverpool and Manchester, the big cities that they were bombing intensively. Our base was an AKAK base: the soldiers' job was to shoot down the planes before they got to their destination. If they didn't get them going over, they would try to get them on the way back.

The German bombers were always escorted by fighter planes for protection. During an attack, the artillery guns would fire at the bombers and the fighters. At night the fighters dove down through the searchlights, shooting machine-gun fire everywhere. The pilots knew that if they could fly under the lights, they could wipe out the searchlight teams.

There was a concrete air-raid shelter about a half block away from the YMCA where we lived. When the sirens went off, we knew the planes were coming or might already be overhead, and we ran for the shelter.

My mom was severely asthmatic. She had emphysema, but in those days they did not know what emphysema was or how to treat it. She was little able to walk half a block without gasping for breath, much less do any physical activity. But one day when the sirens went off she picked up in one hand my brother, and myself in the other, and she ran so fast. Have you ever gone so fast that you felt that maybe only every other foot was touching the ground? Well that's how it seemed to me. I felt as if we were flying through the air in order to get to the air-raid shelter in time. Meanwhile the fighter planes were shooting anything they could find. I wondered how my mother found the strength and courage to physically be able to do that.

On another occasion, we were again alerted to an attack. My father was there, and the whole family started running for the air-raid shelter. I could hear the small planes machine-gunning and the bombs coming down. My father pushed us all the way against the wall and covered us spread-eagle with his body so that we wouldn't get hurt. If anything had come our way it would have hit him first, and he knew that.

Those times really showed me that my family would always be there for me—no matter what it took. It wouldn't matter what I'd done in my life; my parents would always stand by me. No matter what, parents are always there for you.

Laine Johns — *El Paso, Texas*

A Gathering of Strengths

There is a very special person in my life who has given me so much more than I think she even knows: my youngest sister, Toni. Just the other day, I received a phone call from her, and she told me a story about her and her neighbor Linda.

Linda and Toni were good friends, so Toni wasn't surprised to get Linda's telephone call. Each had a ten-year-old son, and that had brought them together. Evan and Eric were in the same class at the school around the corner, and they often played together.

"If you're going to the store today, do you mind if I come with you?" Linda asked.

"Not at all," Toni replied. "I'll come pick you up."

Toni left her house and arrived at Linda's home just a few moments later. Then the pair began their walk to the grocery store a few blocks away. They talked about the weather, their families, and what they might buy at the store.

"Are people staring at us?" Linda asked, and they both laughed. They knew that they were a curious sight. Toni, who had developed arthritis at a young age, was rolling along in her electric wheelchair, while Linda, who was blind, tapped along with her cane, holding on to the arm of Toni's motorized chair.

The two frequently shopped together. It was very convenient: Toni, with her sight, could direct Linda to the items that she needed; Linda, with her mobility, could reach the items on the shelves that Toni couldn't.

"A little to the left. Now back. No, that's raspberry yogurt!" Toni might say as they worked their way around the store. Soon they would make their way to the checkout stand to pay for their groceries, then back home they went, with bags of groceries hanging from Toni's wheelchair.

As I sat listening to my sister's story, I could not help but feel great admiration for these two. They had taken their weaknesses together as one and had turned them into strengths. I feel that this story may very well serve as a lesson to us all. In gathering our weaknesses together, they too may become a greater strength shared for the common good of all mankind.

Kathryn Michel ⏤ Antlers, Oklahoma

The Donkey Cart

One day, things were a mess. We had seven children, ranging from seventeen down to four years old, and they just weren't working together. There were all kinds of bickering and accusations going on.

"He did this and she did that."

"I'm supposed to do this and she won't let me."

"She's supposed to do that and she hasn't yet."

Things were being left undone and things were being half-done. Finally, my husband brought us all into the dining room and sat us down to have a talk.

Now, he's a country boy from back in the woods of southern Georgia and he thinks in country terms. He got out a piece of paper and drew a picture on it.

"This here's an old wagon full of hay and we got to take it where it's supposed to go," he said. "So we're gonna hitch up the team, hitch up the donkeys, the old mules. I'll put two of 'em here on this end, and two of 'em on the back, and two of 'em on this side. There, now we'll hitch 'em up real good. All right, now, we'll get up and go. Where's this wagon goin' to?" The children stared at him.

"Why, it isn't gonna go nowhere," they said. "You got donkeys all over the place going off in different directions."

"That's exactly what's happening in this family," he said. "We're all a bunch of donkeys and we're going every which way. Nobody's doing nothing for the family, and nothing's getting done.

"But what would happen if we put the donkeys at one end, all facing in the same direction? This here wagon is gonna go on down the road. And so is this family if we all pull together," he added.

To this day, every one of our children remembers the story of the donkey cart. It really showed us the need for families to work together.

Mary Lou Mingledorff — Athens, Georgia

Barnstormer's Daughter

It was probably "Lindy," Charles Lindbergh, who most influenced our family's lives. My father was working on an oil rig when Lindbergh's flight across the Atlantic electrified the world. Dad loved flying and decided that he, too, would make his living doing the thing he loved best.

Dad built his own plane. I remember the tiny strips of balsa wood he placed in intricate designs and covered with fabric. He then painted it over and over with layers of what we called "dope." After nine or ten months of work, Dad rolled his creation out onto the prairie, cranked up the motor, and took off!

I took his success for granted because I believed my dad could do anything. Now, I marvel at the fact that the plane actually flew the very first time he tried it. Furthermore, I am now shocked by the fact that, after putting the plane through a few aerobatic maneuvers — stalls and spins — he took each member of the family for a ride. My dad eventually became a barnstormer, or stunt pilot. He became famous for his spectacular stunts — flying low, buzzing houses, and even flying upside down for several minutes at a time.

It was just about this time that Charles Lindbergh made a forced landing in his airplane near our town of Vaughn, New Mexico. My mother happened to be visiting a friend in town who received a phone call asking her to take a box lunch to a stranded pilot. The two women drove to a deserted location where they met a grateful Lindbergh who enthusiastically shook hands with them and thanked them for lunch. There was the celebrated Charles Lindbergh, having a private little rendezvous with my mom out on the New Mexico prairie!

Lindy's stay in Vaughn was extremely short. While the mayor was busily organizing a parade, Lindbergh was busily arranging an escape. Dad identified very strongly with Lindbergh and his exploits; they were kindred spirits, after all. Although at fifteen years old I was much more interested in boys than I was in flying, my dad had plans for me too.

"Any fool can learn to fly," my dad would say. "How about it, gal?"

It never occurred to me that I could "just say no," so my flying lessons began.

Today's student pilots are required to take at least forty hours of ground school instruction, but my education in these subjects took about an hour. Instrument panels in modern aircraft are freckled with dials, but my plane had only three: compass, altimeter, and bank indicator. Two instruments were outside the cabin. Attached to a wing was a triangular-shaped piece of metal, the air-speed indicator. The wind pushed a wire pointer back and forth between its numbers to show the speed. In front of the cabin was the fuel gauge, a little round cap with a wire sticking out of it: when the wire was up, there was gas in the tank; when the wire was down, there was no gas.

When I began flying I paid no attention to the instruments because I already knew where east, south, west, and north were. I soon developed my own system for knowing how high I was, too. When I wanted to land, I looked at the grass growing alongside the runway. When I could distinguish one clump from another, it was time to flare out and land.

Dad had soloed after two or three hours of instruction; by the time I'd had seven or eight, he was ready to retract his theory that "any fool can learn to fly," but he decided to give

me another chance. Today the average student gets ten to twelve hours of flight training before solo flight.

I soloed shortly before my seventeenth birthday, and eventually accumulated enough flying time to apply for a pilot's license. I became one of the five youngest females in the United States to be licensed the following year.

Today, flying is a form of transportation used by many people, but it was a lot different back in those days—it was a lot riskier. The passion for flying that people such as Charles Lindbergh and my father possessed paved the way for the luxury of modern aviation. Being a pioneer takes courage and daring, but it especially requires love and sacrifice.

My father, James Christman, died at the age of forty-seven when his stunt plane went into a spin and crashed before an audience of several thousand: he lived and died for what he truly loved—flying.

Norma L. Jones ▬ *Encinitas, California*

This story is an adaptation from the previously published book, Barnstormer's Daughter, *an autobiography by Norma L. Jones, copyright 1988. Used by permission of the estate of Norma L. Jones.*

A lesson on sharing...

The Crystal Bowl

I was raised in Germany. When World War II ended, I was still a little girl. I lived with my grandmother, my mother, and my two older brothers. My mother had to work all day, but in the evenings she spent time with us. There was not much to do at night because there was no electricity. But we all sat around a big table while Mom lit a kerosene lamp and read exciting stories to us. We almost felt like part of those adventures.

In the middle of the table stood a crystal bowl. My mom always filled it with special treats. Usually there were apples in that bowl, but on one evening the bowl was filled with oranges. Food was hard to come by after the war, and finding oranges for sale was very special. That was the first time I had ever seen an orange.

After my mom read us a story, she took an orange and divided it among us. The whole room started to smell wonderful, and oh, how delicious that orange tasted! When we had finished, we looked longingly at the bowl. Then she gave each of us a whole orange!

My two brothers ate their oranges immediately, but I hesitated. I wanted to save mine for the next day and show the orange to my best friend.

"The choice is yours," Mom told me. "If you eat it now, you can have the whole orange by yourself. But, if you show it to your friend, you will have to share the orange with her."

I could still taste that wonderful flavor, but how could I ever describe it to my friend? And what fun would there be in eating such a treat alone? I decided to share the orange with my girlfriend. The next day, it tasted even better than the night before. We both dreamed of a land where oranges would grow and you could just pick them from a tree.

I brought that crystal bowl with me to California and now it sits on my table. It is always filled with oranges, and if you take one, don't forget to share it with somebody. It is much tastier that way.

Doris Einziger — Danville, California

A lesson on honesty...

Free Rocks

*I*t was show-and-tell day at my granddaughter Katie's third-grade class, and Nathan had brought in his rock collection. Katie had never liked rocks before, but these were different. Nathan had beautiful, polished stones and interesting things like nuggets of fool's gold. She had never seen anything like it, and more than anything Katie wanted to have one of those rocks.

After Nathan had finished sharing his collection, he set it on a side table so the class could view it throughout the day. As the day wore on, Katie's mind focused on only one goal: to get some of those rocks. While everyone was busy, she walked over to the display and pretended to examine the rocks one by one, until she had selected her favorites. She carefully closed her hand over the rocks and carried them back to her desk.

"Now, they are mine," she thought.

After Katie reached home she was finally alone to look at her prize, but the rocks that were once so beautiful now repulsed her. It suddenly hit her that she had stolen something. At school she hadn't thought of it as stealing—she just wanted them, and she figured that Nathan had lots more anyway.

By the next day, Katie couldn't bear to look at the rocks. She just wanted to get rid of them and the guilt she was feeling. She carefully laid the rocks out on the grass in her front yard, with a sign that said "FREE ROCKS." There she sat and waited all day, but no one seemed to want them. Finally, Katie took the rocks and threw them as far as she could, hoping that by throwing those rocks away she could somehow throw away the guilt that she was feeling.

Although Katie never confessed to Nathan that she stole his rocks, to this day she remembers her first and last episode of stealing—she had never felt so unhappy. She didn't even enjoy what she had taken because of the guilt of knowing it was wrong.

I think Katie was lucky to learn this lesson at a young age: don't take other people's property. Being honest gives you peace of mind and allows you to be happy and to always feel good about yourself.

Joan Calder — San Diego, California

What No One Can Take Away

I don't want to go to school. I hate homework," I complained. It was very important in my family to get good grades, but at nine years old I didn't want to study so hard. When Grandmother Lipschitz heard my words, she pulled me aside. She was very elegant as she chided me in a somber manner.

"Your education is so important," Nanny said. "You need to do the very best you can in school because that will stay with you for the rest of your life. No one can ever take that away from you, and that will help you to survive."

Fanny Lipschitz was born into a Jewish family in Russia. She was the only daughter of a wealthy furrier; her father sold furs to make coats, muffs, and hats for the cold Russian winters. As a little girl, her life was very simple and carefree. Her favorite pastime was watching their pastry chef create tasty marvels of flaky dough.

Then trouble began. People who hated them because of their beliefs started pogroms, or attacks, on Jewish families. They went around in mobs, looting and destroying homes and businesses. The government did not try to stop them. My great-grandfather was able to escape to Germany, but Fanny had to stay behind with her small sons, Max and Michael. Fanny and Max were put in jail because she would not say where her father had gone.

Finally, they were released. Though their house had been looted, she was able to save the family jewels which had been hidden among some rags in the kerosene lamps. The mobs had tossed aside the old lanterns, thinking them of little value.

Nanny and her sons escaped by horse-drawn carriage to Moscow, then proceeded to Leipzig, Germany, to join her father. By then he had established himself in business and was prospering once more. For a while their life was very good, until Adolf Hitler came into power. Then life in Germany became worse than it ever had been in Russia. Thousands of Jews were being imprisoned and put to death in the Holocaust. My grandmother was able to escape to America after my father had set sail on a ship to Palestine to participate in the Maccabbean games. Many family members disappeared, never to be seen again.

My grandmother, Fanny, had never worked before she came to America, but after her arrival she knew she would need to work to survive. She put on her hat and her white gloves and went from door to door seeking employment as a lady's maid. To her amazement, she was refused each time.

"What is wrong?" she finally asked. "Why will no one hire me?"

"You are more of a lady than I am," Nanny was told. "I would be very uncomfortable having you wait on me."

My grandmother took boarders into her own apartment, providing meals and a clean place to sleep. In time, she was able to save enough money to buy a chicken farm in New Jersey, which she ran with her own hands. Fanny Lipschitz was a remarkable woman. So much had been taken away, but each time she started over. I will never forget her words:

"Get a good education. No one can ever take that away from you."

Marion Sciré — *Coronado, California*

Severe Brothers Saddlery

*I*n September, when cowboys came into town for the big Pendleton rodeo, they often bunked at our house. Our family lived in the bottom floor of a former World War II army barrack. The cowboys stayed upstairs, where my dad had a saddle shop—right next to the sign "Severe Brothers Saddlery," someone had put up another sign that read "Hotel de Cowpunch" in big letters.

It was interesting to sit in Dad's shop after a long day of rodeo and watch the cowboys compare bruises. They'd swap stories and practice roping the dummy steer in the corner made from a bale of hay covered with canvas. Perhaps they came there for inspiration: everybody knew that the grand prize for the top cowboy at the Pendleton Roundup was a Severe Brothers saddle.

I spent hours watching my dad and my uncle make saddles in that shop. I loved the rich smells of cowhide and sheepskin, with the tang of sawdust mixed in. When I was small, I used to curl up in Dad's big box of sheepskins and fall asleep to the sounds of the buzzing bandsaw, the tapping of mallets, and the "scritch, scritch" of the blade as my uncle scraped hides.

Severe Brothers saddles were totally made from scratch. Uncle Bill made the tree, or wooden frame of the saddle, the part that actually forms the shape. He started with a block of wood, cutting it with the bandsaw to just the right size. Often the floor of the tree room would be ten inches deep in sawdust.

Uncle Bill used cattle skins, purchased from a meat-packing company, to cover the tree. After he had soaked the hides and scraped off all the hair, he stretched the wet rawhide leather over the wooden tree and stitched it together. As the leather dried, it became very taut and strong.

My father turned the saddle trees into beautiful fin-ished saddles. In one area of the shop there was a long, extra-wide table for sheets of leather to be laid out and cut — flat cardboard patterns hung on the wall above it. My father cut out the pieces of leather, then tooled or decorated them. Dad became very skilled at making elaborate designs. He chose the tool that had the desired pattern on it, and when he tapped it on the leather, it left a permanent imprint. It might take him three months to complete one saddle, depending on how intricate the tooling work was.

Next, Dad attached the leather pieces to the tree. I can still picture him with a mouthful of tacks, quickly tapping them into the leather. In some places—such as attaching the sheepskin to the bottom of the saddle—Dad used a big sewing machine that could sew the toughest leather. When he finished, I was amazed to see a beautiful saddle, that had started out as mere wood and cattle skins. From beginning to end Dad made sure each saddle was the very best. He had very high standards, and after many years he became so expert at his craft, that his saddles became famous for their quality.

Watching my father work has made me appreciate handcrafted items; it takes a lot of time and skill to make something by hand. Nowadays it seems that nearly everything is mass-produced by machines, but you can always tell when something is handmade. I learned from my father to appreciate quality work; when I do something, I try to do it the very best I can.

Billy Dawn Severe-Lohman ⏤ *Rancho Bernardo, California*

Duff Severe is the only saddlemaker whose work is recognized and displayed by the Smithsonian Institution. As a skilled craftsman, he has also received a National Heritage Fellowship from the National Endowment of the Arts, and he has been featured by the National Geographic Society both in their magazine and on their television program. Perhaps an ad for Wrangler Jeans states it best: the caption below a photo of Duff Severe reads, "The Legend in Jeans."

The Carpenter

*A*s I sit down with my grandson, Jon, to discuss a story that he wrote about my husband, I reflect on how we loved and continue to love our grandchildren. We did the easiest and most difficult thing in life for the past thirty years: we dared to love our grandchildren as our own at the risk of personal sacrifice. And in the end, we benefited from the richness of unconditional love—risking nothing that did not matter. Here is the story my grandson Jon Murray wrote to illustrate my point:

It should have been no surprise to me that my grandfather would bring me luck even from the grave. If anyone could trick death it would be him. Although Grandpa never gave me a pot of gold, three wishes, or any other Irish mythical rewards, he did sit in the hard aluminum bleachers enduring the scorching summer sun to watch his eight-year-old grandson play baseball. He did this until I graduated from high school. Grandpa was at every football, basketball, and baseball game. He made it to every music recital and award banquet. He bought my first clarinet and oil-painting kit. This from a carpenter who ran away from home in the early 1900s so that he would not have to follow in his father's footsteps. His father had dug coal from the West Virginia mountainside only to die poor and with lungs filled with black soot.

Grandpa was my father when my parents divorced. He spent hours over the years telling me stories of "Little People" who would sneak into our bedrooms at nights to tie our shoelaces in knots or steal our socks.

"These Little People didn't mean any harm," he said. "So we shouldn't be afraid. It's just their way of keeping life interesting." Whenever I needed something, my grandfather always seemed to find a way to help. I don't know how because we were all poor.

"Poor in riches, but not in love or spirit," I hear him telling me even now. But I can tell you, we were "poor in riches." And when I wanted to play clarinet in the school band, it seemed like magic that the week after I told Grandpa this he brought home a new clarinet for me to play. The only payment he required was that I sit with him and listen to Benny Goodman and his orchestra play during one summer afternoon. He did the same for baseball gloves, bats, shoes, coats, and God knows what else a kid who wants to be like every other kid could want. I never stopped to ask him how he got these things for me. To me he was my "Irish Luck" and that was good enough.

At his funeral it surprised me that so many strangers were there to pay their respects to the man who was my grandfather. In retrospect, I know most of these people were the ones that my grandfather was able to convince to strike a deal or barter a trade for the things his grandson needed; perhaps the only reason they did so was because Grandpa was so honest and his love was so true. Love and truth persuaded many business persons in our small northern California town to make an economic exchange with my grandfather that made no economic sense.

At the site of his burial in the hills around Wiskeytown Lake one day, under tall pine trees blowing in the Indian summer breeze and amidst the laughing sound of the creek nearby, I looked up into the sky and asked God if Grandpa was still with me. I need to know, God, I said, because he was my good luck and my laughter. And even though I didn't expect a visitation—it wasn't Grandpa's style!—or a booming voice from the heavens, couldn't I have some small sign that Grandpa was still making deals for me up there? After a few moments of silence I decided that my sign would not come today. I started back to my car when a rock by the stream caught my attention. I looked down and saw a small, smooth granite rock that had a white quartz ring in the shape of a heart! I ran back to where my mother and older brother had been and told them about my discovery. We stood in disbelief as the wind swirled around the tall pines and three suddenly very small people. That rock was sign enough for me that my Irish Luck was still there. As a testament that goodness and love do prevail, even beyond the grave, to this day I have that stone in my office as a reminder of my grandfather.

I didn't know how much he meant to me until after his death. It's been more than ten years now since he died, and I feel so much older. But it's true that goodness, honesty, and sincerity are the things that will endure throughout our individual struggles and pain. These are the things that my daughter and son will learn. And I, too, will sit on the hot steel bleachers, yell at the top of my lungs at the end of the school play, and sit at the piano to play a tune with my children after a long workday—all because a genius of a man did the same for me.

Madge Stone — Redding, California

© 1966 Jon Murray

Through the Eyes of a Child

I hate bugs! I shiver at the thought of any creepy, crawling, buzzing, annoying "thing" near me. I particularly dislike spiders!

One morning, my four-year-old granddaughter and I saw a huge daddy longlegs spider in the grass. I was ready to run away, but Claudia stooped down to watch. Before I could say "Ugh," she said, "Look, it's Inky-Dinky." Claudia had learned the song "The Itsy-Bitsy Spider" at nursery school, only to her it was "Inky-Dinky."

After I stopped shivering with dread, I stood beside her as she tried to catch the spider. I discovered some interesting things about that daddy longlegs; one of the spider's many legs is longer than the others, and he uses it as an antenna, feeling what's ahead. He can go backward, forward, and sideways very quickly. Suddenly, this ugly, nasty creature became amusing, amazing—it now was a being, with a secret life of its own. How many other things and beings had I overlooked because I was too busy or not interested?

When raising my own children, I either didn't have the time or I was too tired to stop and play with them and notice such things. But the precious time spent with my granddaughter makes me concentrate on the now. She brings me into her world, a world that as a grown-up I have forgotten— a world of trust and wonder, anticipation and excitement. I feel young again, looking through the eyes of a child.

When Claudia grows up, I hope that she will never be too busy or feel too tired to enjoy the wonder of life and living. The world is beautiful and fascinating if we will only take the time to observe, to stop and smell the roses.

Theresa Frankiewicz ⏤ Magnolia, New Jersey

Full House

"Not another stranger!" said Grandma Allen.

"Don't do it, Reba, let the city take care of him," said Uncle Ben.

"Where are we going to put him?" asked Aunt Hope, in despair.

There was a moment of silence. Where were we going to put him? My dad had brought home another stray, only it was not a cat: It was the oldest, most decrepit man I had ever seen in my life. He was pale and so ill he could hardly walk. He shouldn't be left out on the streets, but I didn't want him to die in our house either. Yet I knew that once Dad had made up his mind to do a thing, there was no changing it. Oh, where to put him?

We lived in a three-story house on a quiet street in Edgewood, Rhode Island. Actually, we only lived on the second floor. My parents and I—I was an only child—were squeezed into that single level with my two bedridden grandmothers. Through the years, various aunts and uncles also came and went, and they were always welcomed.

Mrs. Crocker had the third floor. My father had known her husband and when he died she had no place to go. "Don't worry," he said, "we have plenty of room," and he gave her the entire floor.

Charley hung out on the first floor. It held the living areas—the kitchen, the dining room, the parlor, etc. My father had found Charley on the streets with no work and no place to go, so he offered him a place to live in exchange for housecleaning. Dad probably thought that would be a help to Mother; alas, she followed Charley around wringing her hands as he lazily sloshed the floors with a mop and dropped cigarette ash on the Persian rugs. Mother also had to cook for him. I don't know what Dad was thinking; you could tell by looking at Charley that he ate a lot of food.

The only empty place we had left was the cellar, but even a cellar was better than living out in the cold. That's where the old man went, and my mother just added another plate to the table.

Mother never complained. She had beautiful hands and in her younger days had been a pianist at the theater where Dad worked as projectionist. In that era of silent movies, she had provided emotion and excitement on the piano, with pounding chords and dramatic runs up and down the keyboard. Now her hands just cooked and cleaned, cleaned and cooked, but she never seemed to mind. Her favorite expression was, "Cheer up!"

Our family didn't have a lot of money to spare, but what we had we always shared. Although we weren't wealthy, we were sure happy. My parents taught me that giving makes you happy. It didn't matter why people were down and out; Dad brought them home and Mother took them in.

Dorothy Sheldon ⏤ San Diego, California

Fleeing From Pancho Villa

I t was 1918, and my husband's grandfather, Miguel Duarte, had seen enough of the killing and ugliness that goes with war. He had joined Pancho Villa's army during the Mexican Revolution, because he believed that victory would bring democracy to his country, then ruled by dictators. Grandfather was a simple farmer, but a very hard worker. He wanted his wife and five children to enjoy a happy, peaceful life.

However, Grandfather was no longer sure that the cause he was fighting for was the answer to his country's problems. Once he had felt that the war was right and just, but day after day the constant fighting and death brought despair, and he wanted no more of it. Grandfather confided his feelings to another rebel soldier who felt the same way. They decided to ride their horses out of camp in the middle of the night and return to their families. They knew the penalty for deserting Pancho Villa's army: death! Nevertheless, Grandfather was determined to gather his family in Chihuahua, Mexico, and take them across the border to safety in the United States.

Finally, the right night arrived and the two men jumped on their horses and galloped away from camp as fast as they could. They were quickly discovered missing, and Pancho Villa sent several soldiers out to capture them. When Grandfather and his companion realized that they were being pursued, they pushed their horses as hard as they could. Riding a horse so

quickly across rough country was exhausting to both rider and horse, as well as being very dangerous. Soon Grandfather's companion had had enough, and the man begged Grandfather to give up. He would not, and he went on alone. Later, he learned that his companion had been shot in front of everyone in camp, as a warning to the other men against desertion.

Grandfather's horse was tiring quickly, so he dismounted and hid behind some large rocks by the sloping side of a creek bed. Hiding there in the dark of night, his heart pounded with fright. As the soldiers traveled back and forth searching for him, he saw the sparks fly from their horses' hooves as they struck the rocks along the creekbed.

Grandfather did escape that night, and traveling by foot, he came within a few miles of his home in Chihuahua. Little did he know that soldiers had also been sent to Chihuahua and were in the village searching for him at that very moment.

As Grandfather neared the outskirts of the town, he saw a strange person approaching him on the trail.

"Do not go home yet," the curious individual told Grandfather.

Although Grandfather had never seen the man before, he obeyed. He waited an extra day, then entered Chihuahua, gathered his family together, and fled to the United States.

To his dying day, my husband's grandfather always believed that it was an angel who warned him of the danger. And you know what? We also believe it. Today, we do not face revolution, war, or threats of death, but Miguel Duarte's love for his family, his courage, and his spirituality have inspired us to have courage in our trials, too.

Donna Gonzales — Poway, California

The City of Angels

magine, if you can, waking up at 4:31 a.m. to the deafening sound of what seems like an Amtrak train going through your house and destroying all that it finds in its path. But on January 17, 1994, it wasn't a train; instead, we awoke to a massive earthquake that registered 6.7 on the Richter scale.

We were scared, but the darkness that surrounded us made the experience more devastating—we couldn't tell what had happened to our house. My husband, Roberto, had put flashlights in an easy-to-find place, but when we went to get them, they were not there. Later, we found them amid the debris that covered the floor.

We had a crank radio for use in emergencies, and after awhile, Roberto got it to work, but no one knew much at that point. Meanwhile, more and more temblors followed, and we were more preoccupied with getting under the frame of a door than in hearing the news.

When the sun came up, we saw that the kitchen floor was covered, wall-to-wall, with broken glass. The cabinets had opened and many of our dishes were on the floor in pieces. The water from the tap was polluted and came out in a brown gush, and the electricity had gone out. The loss of electricity, even though it was daylight, left us in the dark as to the devastation surrounding us. We didn't even have a newspaper for a couple of days, since that building, too, was badly damaged.

The best thing we did was go out of our home and reach out to those in need. There was so much to do. We were especially needed because we speak Spanish, and many of those who were the most heavily affected were also Spanish-speaking. In their own countries, they had been taught to seek open spaces during earthquakes, and many were camping out in parks.

When I was asked by a lieutenant of the Salvation Army to go and tell them to come to the shelters that were prepared for them, I could not believe what I saw. There were thousands of hungry people living out in the cold winter air. Many children were sick with the flu. How rewarding it was to offer them shelter where they would be helped to get on their feet again.

No longer were we afraid; we didn't have time for such things. Others needed us more. Sure, we paused as we felt the continuing aftershocks, but we kept on. What a blessing it was to be serving others so we could stop worrying about our own situation.

When the newspapers started again, I found this article. It was written by the owners of a heavily damaged store, The Broadway*:

Now We Know Why They Call It the City of Angels

Early on Monday, the earth moved—and plunged greater Los Angeles into terror and darkness.

Then the angels came out.

Some were easy to recognize: Fire, police, paramedics, medical personnel, and all those whose job it is to be angels, every day.

But countless others wore no uniform. They were the angels who, as strangers, teamed to rescue people, pets, and possessions. Who offered whatever they could to folks they'd never met. Who flooded radio and TV stations with calls asking how to help. Who wrapped their arms around a person in tears.

Suddenly, angels are everywhere.

And as we watch, a city wrenched apart has begun pulling together again.

It will be a slow, painful healing, but the Los Angeles that arises will be a stronger and more united community than ever before.

Thanks to all the angels.

Hilda Gandola — *West Hills, California*

* *Permission to reprint courtesy of Macy's, a part of Federated Department Stores, Inc.*

Joyful Sight

*I*t was evening. My daughter Kristin and her family had just returned from a shopping trip and it was time for three-and-a-half-year-old Brian to go to bed. As they mounted the stairs, Kristin saw that Brian was playing with a twenty-four-inch rod from a newly purchased shelving set. Sensing danger, she asked Brian to give her the rod. His stubborn three-year-old response was "No."

Just then, the end of the rod hit the stair above where Brian was stepping and shot back into his right eye like an arrow. Kristin rushed him to the hospital where he underwent a five-hour operation. Although the lens was destroyed, doctors were able to save his injured eye. They were certain that with time and proper healing, an artificial lens would allow him full vision.

Meanwhile, Brian became fully conscious, feeling confused and very angry. He found himself in strange surroundings, with a bandaged and painful eye. In response to the pain and fear, Brian refused to open his uninjured eye. It was his way of taking a small measure of control over a truly frightening situation.

"There is nothing wrong with your left eye," we reasoned with him, but he wouldn't listen. His parents took him to a toy store and offered to buy any toy he saw if he would open his eye and choose one. They threatened to take away his beloved trains; nothing worked. I couldn't blame him.

I have often been afraid and I have wanted nothing more than to close my eyes and shut out the world.

Four days later, at our request, the doctor gently pulled the eyelids open to prove to Brian that he could still see with his uninjured eye. At first Brian wouldn't open it on his own, but gradually, over several days, he began to ease the eye open. Then he became so excited to see again that he wanted to see everything.

"Grandma," Brian called, "Come up to my bedroom, Grandma."

I followed him up the stairs to his room. There he proceeded to run from one toy to another, laughing and showing each to me. When we had exhausted all the objects in his room, he pulled me into his sister Danielle's room. There he gleefully examined and showed me all of her possessions. Exhausted from this burst of activity and the excitement of regaining half of his vision, he asked me to lie down beside him on his bed. I laid down and he curled up against me. He then reached back and patted me, saying, "Grandma, you are my friend."

This painful experience was something we wish had not happened, yet out of it came a rare and beautiful moment of joy. Who can say that the triumph is not worth the pain? By overcoming his fears and opening his eye, Brian regained a world he thought was lost.

Sometimes we try to deny our problems, but they never really go away. If instead we have the courage to open our eyes and face difficulties, we can overcome them. In our triumph we'll regain a world of joy.

Joanna Taylor ⏵ *Santee, California*

Doctor Porter

My son is the sixth generation of medical doctors in our family. The first Dr. Porter graduated from Transylvania Medical School in Kentucky in 1840, as did several of his brothers. His son also became a doctor, and served in the Civil War. The fourth Dr. Porter was my father, John Richard Porter. He played basketball for Indiana University and earned a place in the Indiana Basketball Hall of Fame in New Castle, before graduating from Indiana University's Medical School in 1918.

When my father became a doctor, he had very strong ideas about helping others. Patients would come to his office, located in an old house, and since he didn't have a nurse or a receptionist, they just sat and waited until it was their turn. When it was time, the patient came and sat next to Daddy's desk. He examined them, decided upon a treatment, and then went into a back room and brought out the medicine.

Many of the people in the town were poor, but there were also those who were rich. Rich or poor, he charged everyone the same amount: twenty-five cents for the visit and twenty-five cents for medicine. His old desk was always piled high with quarters. When poor families needed something extra—an operation, their tonsils removed, a baby delivered, or a broken arm set—they often could not afford to pay. Daddy always let them work off the bill by doing the wash and ironing for our family, mowing the yard, or cleaning the gutters.

Here was a man who came from a long line of doctors and could have been very wealthy. Instead, our family was not wealthy, and Daddy worked so hard that he decided to retire early at the age of fifty. He believed that it was more important to serve others than to make lots of money.

After many years of retirement, Daddy contracted leukemia. Even then he insisted upon giving so much of himself for others. He allowed other doctors to experiment on him, using new drugs to try to find a cure. Often when we went to visit Daddy, the flesh on his body was peeling because of the effects of those drugs.

My father got his philosophy of caring for others from his father, his grandfather, and his great-grandfather. Through his example of lifelong service to others, he has passed that legacy on to his children and his grandchildren.

Susan Smith — *Louisville, Kentucky*

Great-Grandpa's Wallpaper

*M*y grandmother's father had become a very wealthy man. He started out in business as a tinker, selling items from a little cart. By working hard and investing his money, he eventually came to own a whole block of stores in Illinois, including a cinema. Unfortunately, much of Great-Grandfather's money was invested in stocks, and when the stock market crashed in 1929, the stocks became worthless. Almost overnight, he lost most of his wealth.

Although many of my great-grandfather's friends became very depressed, he had a great sense of humor. He figured rich or poor, he could still be happy. As a joke, he took his worthless stock certificates and used them to wallpaper the walls of his office. There he would sit with his friends and laugh about his wealth, which now decorated his walls.

Years later, after Great-Grandfather's death, his sons looked at those papers and thought that maybe they might be worth something after all. The brothers steamed the certificates off the walls and redeemed them. They were indeed very valuable; from the sale of those stocks there was enough money to buy every child in the family—there were six of them—a house.

I admire my great-grandfather's spirit. He felt that the loss of the money was just one of those things that happen.

With or without the stocks, his life went on. It goes to show that you should never give up. No matter how bad things seem at the moment, if you endure, they do get better.

Toni Owen — San Diego, California

Injustice

I remember as a little girl in Kentucky going downtown with my mother to the five-and-dime store. They had a soda counter there that quickly drew my attention away from all the other wonders the store offered. Well, I pestered my mother to death until finally she went to the counter and ordered ice cream cones. My dad was waiting in the car, so she bought two, one for me and one for her. At first the salesgirl didn't notice me standing there because I was so small I didn't come up to the counter. But when she returned, she reached over and saw me.

"I'm sorry. We can't sell to Coloreds," the salesgirl said. My mother was very fair-skinned and often was mistaken as being Caucasian. The salesgirl hadn't realized she was Black. Well, Mother just lost it. She threw the two ice cream cones, hitting a mirror, and knocking all the stacked glasses to the floor. Then she began shouting at the girl. I was so scared to see her get that angry; I didn't really understand what was going on, but I knew something very bad had happened. I ran out the door.

By then my father had heard the commotion. He had just gotten out of the car when my mother came raging out of the store, looking for something to throw through the store window. Dad just picked her right up, put her over his shoulder, and carried her quietly to the car.

My mother was still very upset as we drove home. World War II was being fought at that time, and she had several nephews serving abroad. We had not received mail from them for months, and she was very concerned.

"My nephews may be dead in Europe," she said, "fighting for a country that wouldn't even serve them ice cream." My father agreed that it was wrong and greatly unfair.

"But how silly to get that angry and upset," he told her. "What did it accomplish?" He insisted that anger would not help matters at all; there are much better ways to change the world. Time proved that he was right.

About a month later, a mass meeting was held for people of all races to come together to work out problems. At that meeting, the manager of the five-and-dime store came forward, and publicly apologized.

"It is not our policy to discriminate," the man said. "That salesgirl was wrong—we will serve people of any skin color. And if anyone knows who the lady is whose feelings have been hurt, please apologize for me."

My father was there as well as some others in the audience who knew my mother. When she heard of the apology, she did feel much better.

That experience has stayed with me. I taught my own children that they really need to stay in control of their emotions, no matter what, no matter how they've been wronged. So much can happen in a split second of rage to put a person in danger. And what does it accomplish? There are much better ways to deal with injustice.

Annisue Briggs – *Hopkinsville, Kentucky*

An Act of Love

It was January 12, 1996, when Sarah and Sarahi entered the world in Tijuana, Mexico. Their parents knew they were going to add twins to the four other children already at home, but they did not know that the twins were conjoined. Conjoined, or Siamese twins, are identical twins whose bodies are joined together when they are born, usually at the hip, chest, or head. Because they often share organs, one — sometimes both — infants can die during or shortly after birth.

Sanatorrio Santa Maria Hospital, where the babies were born, was a very small hospital and could not care for them, and it seemed nobody else would accept them either.

"Nobody, nobody, nobody," exclaimed the hospital administrator.

Finally, doctors at Children's Hospital in San Diego were asked by a family member if they could help the twins. Without hesitation, a five-member team from Children's Hospital went to pick up the babies and their mother by ambulance. Although the twins were not covered by insurance and the father earns less than fifty dollars a week, doctors proceeded to help the family by separating the conjoined sisters.

"This surgery," said Dr. Lamberti, Director of the Children's Heart Institute, "is [as complicated as] a moonshot or shuttle launch. We need to have everything well-understood and it must be timed like a ballet."

The surgeons knew that without the surgery, neither twin had a chance to survive. The medical team of more than thirty surgeons, heart specialists, nurses, and others, staged a dress rehearsal of the intricate surgery the night before. They sewed together store-bought dolls about the same size as the twins to use in the practice run. Meanwhile, the mother and father prayed that the daughters God had allowed them to bring into the world would both be able to go home with them.

This was not to be the case for Sarahi, the weaker of the sisters. After many hours of surgery, doctors realized that she was not able to live without her twin's stronger organs. However, even after Sarahi's death, she helped Sarah to survive: portions of Sarahi's ribs and skin were later used to close the gap left in Sarah's chest by the surgery. In later years, Sarah will grow to appreciate this gift from her sister.

This act of love was made possible by people who saw a need and ran to the rescue: doctors gave their time around the clock, nurses and staff never blinked at the extra weekend hours, the Ronald McDonald House housed the family, and Nordstrom dressed both babies in their finest clothes. All this effort to save a precious little life. It didn't matter that these babies were from Mexico, only that they were children in desperate need. This is America; this is what we stand for.

— *Anonymous*

Christmas in Alaska

I love Christmas, with a brightly lit tree and lots of presents for everyone. But the Christmases that I love best were during the winters our family spent in Alaska. In 1957, my husband and I took our two small children, Randy and Laciene, to homestead near Susitna Station along the Susitna River in Alaska. The place was so far away from stores and the city that we had to learn to make nearly everything with our own hands and our own wits. Because the weather was so cold, the decisions we made often meant the difference between life and death.

Our children learned to work very hard, but it was lots of fun. One of their jobs was caring for the dog teams. Our dogs were very important. They were our protection and our doorbell, barking at any approaching animals or people. During the long winter they were our sole transportation.

Sometimes during the holidays we hitched up our two dog-sled teams and went to visit our neighbors at Flathorn Lake. Although it was only ten miles away, it took most of a day for the trip, as we skidded along under the Northern Lights.

One winter the weather was really bad. An airplane usually came out once a week to bring mail to us. That year there were so many storms that the planes couldn't come. We had ordered toys for the children as Christmas presents, but it didn't look like they would arrive in time.

"What are we going to do for Christmas?" I wondered. Well, the children's grandfather was a carpenter, and he lived only a few miles away. He made a beautiful little wooden cradle for Laciene's doll, and a brightly painted wagon for Randy. Since we didn't have tree decorations, we did old-fashioned things—popping and stringing corn, and making ornaments from little bits of paper that the children cut out. We made all kinds of wonderful things.

Just as we got everything together, the plane came in and brought their Christmas presents! That was a nice ending, but I knew that those toys didn't make it a real Christmas. It was the love of our family, and the time that we spent working and playing together that brought the Christmas spirit—we didn't need the material things to make us happy.

Audie Glazebrook ⟶ Aztec, New Mexico

Lilacs

Whenever I see the lilacs bloom, I remember the springtime when I was five years old. I had caught pneumonia—it was Balther pneumonia—and I was in bed for a very long time. I was the tenth child out of twelve, and everyone was so kind to me.

I was put on a folding bed in the front parlor. My mother placed two quart jars filled with hot water under the blankets, to get me to perspire. One day, Mother brought me a shoebox filled with lilacs—they were blooming so beautifully at that time of the year. She had poked holes in the lid of the box with a nail to spell my name, "Leona." I'd take the blossoms off the stems and put them in the holes—it looked so pretty to see my name spelled out in flowers.

Each day Mother brought me fresh lilacs. There was no television in those days, so it gave me something to do while I was so ill. When I had children I did the same thing for them. If I didn't have lilacs, I would use other flowers, and soon it became a family tradition.

Little things that show we care can make all the difference in a family. Sometimes it's the little things that we remember most.

Leona Parsons ⁓ Paso Robles, California

A lesson on being dependable...

Life in Africa

I grew up in the countryside of Sierra Leone, in Africa. Rural living was very simple, quiet, and sometimes strenuous, but I did not realize it until I experienced more comfortable living. Nonetheless, I learned a lot of valuable lessons from growing up in the country.

We went to bed with the chickens and had to be up when they crowed—they were our alarm clock. Every child had chores to do, and the number-one chore was getting water for the household. Containers for carrying water were sized according to one's age, and as a teenager, I could easily carry a bucket with over three gallons of water on my head. One does not practice this skill—you grow up with it.

The open well was about one and a half miles from our home. We rushed to get there early to get clean water, for the constant dipping of buckets into the well caused the water to become very muddy for latecomers. Early in the morning, one could hear children's voices, like birds, and the clanking of bucket with bucket as we hurried to get clean water. We made at least four trips each day; all walking was done bare-footed and on ten toes.

The next duty was to heat bathing water for the adults in a big pot over the fire. The fire would light quicker if one got hot coals from a neighbor who had already begun theirs; hence, everyone lingered before starting their fires! The water had to be at a boiling point before it was poured into an aluminum bucket and carried to the washroom. The adults took turns bathing, with the men usually going first. Many times, it being the tropics, baths were taken twice daily — mornings and before going to bed.

The brushing of teeth was another important task. In Sierra Leone, there are special trees from which sticks are broken to be used as toothbrushes. One end of the stick is chewed on until it makes a strong bristle that brushes teeth very clean and makes them feel very fresh. Some people brushed their teeth with charcoal by just rubbing the teeth hard with a used coal from the fire.

Another duty was sweeping, inside and outside, around the house. Brooms were made from palm or coconut branches, with several stalks tied together. Every child owned one. After sweeping, we did our regular dusting. Dust accumulated quickly there, particularly when dry winds blew from the Sahara — clothes and furniture were constantly covered with dust.

We also did the laundry. This was done by the river about two miles away. We did not have many clothes, but those we had were laundered weekly. We dipped the garments into the water and then laid them on a rock. We applied soap to each piece, then combined several garments and pounded them on the rock three times with both hands; some people used a bat for pounding. After several poundings, the garments were again dipped in the water and rinsed. The rocks were sometimes halfway in the water so one had to stand in the river for a long time, knee high. One day my sister came out of the water with a blue watersnake wrapped around her foot! The watersnake was very playful and harmless, and it quickly slid off her foot as she ran away.

Nature seemed to have put rocks by the banks of the river just for this service. In fact, one who was very reliable and dependable was usually called a "waterside stone." Those rocks are always there, waiting to do their duty.

As a child in a rural village, one had to be very reliable because the work one did was very important to one's family. We learned to be "waterside stones." Learning to work hard is one of the blessings of rural breeding.

Zainabu Renner ⟶ *Decatur, Georgia*

The Runaway Statue of Liberty

*T*he Fourth of July was a big day in my little hometown of Mink Creek, Idaho. It was Picnic Day, Patriotic Program Day, Chocolate-Cake-and-Homemade-Ice-Cream-at-the-Park Day. Then one year it also became Parade Day.

We'd never had a parade before, but since ours was a farming community we had plenty of horse-drawn haywagons to decorate as floats. Some floats would depict scenes from the early history of our country. The Singing Mothers would ride on another float warbling "The Battle Hymn of the Republic," while horses pulled them around the park. But the most important part of the whole parade would be the Statue of Liberty float; the Statue of Liberty symbolized everything our country stood for.

I wanted to be the Statue of Liberty, dressed in a flowing white robe and holding aloft the flaming torch — just orange cellophane, but it almost looked real. The Statue would ride on a decorated milk cart pulled by one pure white horse. It was going to be a magic, exciting day, and I wanted to be part of it, but my cousin Carolyn, blond and beautiful, was chosen to be the Statue.

I hoped I would at least get to carry the flag that led the parade, but one of the boys was picked to do that. I was too young to be Betsy Ross, and too old to march with the little kids beating drums made from oatmeal boxes, so what was there left for me to do?

To my dismay, I was asked to carry one of the two poles that held up the sign, "George Washington, Our First President." I wouldn't even have a costume, just blue jeans and a white blouse with a red tie around my neck. Who would notice a pole carrier, dressed in blue jeans? I would be unimportant, invisible. Who needed me?

On the morning of the parade, we lined up in a farmyard across from the park. We could see the grandstand, full of people from our little town and the surrounding villages. They would all cheer for my cousin Carolyn on her Statue of Liberty float, and for the flag carrier and the Singing Mothers, but who would cheer for me?

It was almost time for the parade to start. A few people who had band instruments were going to march and play the music while the Singing Mothers sang. The white horse pulling the Statue of Liberty's float was nervous as the band tuned up; he danced around, and the driver had a hard time calming him. Some of the Singing Mothers were late and a couple of little kids began to cry. Things were not going well.

I looked at the whole line-up of the parade and wished I could disappear. In the bright morning light there was no magic. The flag hung limp from its long pole, and the Statue of Liberty's flame was only cellophane, after all. George Washington's white wig was just wads of cotton, and the oatmeal-box band was dumb.

Finally, the parade began. As the band blew its first notes and the Singing Mothers trilled, "Mine eyes have seen the glory," the white horse bolted. Startled by the music, he ran out of the farmyard and down the road, the milk-cart float bumping along behind him. We all watched as the Statue of Liberty, valiantly holding her torch aloft, disappeared in a cloud of dust.

"Catch them!" somebody yelled.

The parade dispersed as we all pursued the runaway horse, people pouring out of the grandstand and down the road. Suddenly we all had a new purpose, to save the Statue of Liberty. A man on horseback managed to turn the runaway float around, and the horse ran back toward us, still yanking the milk cart with the Statue clinging to its sides. As the white horse drew closer, George Washington and Betsy Ross stood shoulder-to-shoulder with the Singing Mothers, the oatmeal box band and me in a blockade to stop him when he got to us. Fortunately, the horse was calm by then and the Statue of Liberty was safe. But standing there with the others gave me time to realize something — we had all stood together to try to save Miss Liberty.

"That's what it's all about," I thought to myself, "standing together against a danger." That's what George Washington and Betsy Ross and all of our other forefathers and foremothers had done so many years before. They had built a country where each of us was important and valuable, where it took all of us to make it work, whether we carried the flag or just toted a pole at the end of the parade.

"Let's start," my cousin Carolyn said as she raised her torch high again. The magic was back: the flame burned brightly; a slight breeze fluttered the flag; the band played; and the Singing Mothers sang, "Mine eyes have seen the glory..." The kids with the oatmeal box drums beat them steadily, "Pum, pum, pum-pum-pum." As the parade moved forward, I hoisted my side of the First President of Our Country banner. I was part of it all, and my heart beat strong with pride.

Lael Littke ━ Pasadena, California

Tough and Tender

Somehow Grandma Suzie demanded respect. What made us revere her so? What caused the mellow, melting feeling I still get when I think of her some forty years after her death?

I grew up in the house next door to my grandmother. Her given name was Suzanne, but to the grandchildren — my brother and me — she was Grandma Suzie. She was the example that molded our lives.

"People don't get old and tough, they get old and tender," she often said with disdain. But she was tough — as tough as the rooster she threatened to dismember when he barred her entry to the henhouse for the daily egg-gathering.

Her hands were gnarled and showed the brown spots of aging. However, there was no tenderness in her grip on the hoe when she smote the weeds in her vegetable garden, nothing gentle in her fingers as she pounded and kneaded the bread dough.

She plunged into life. All four feet nine of her dared a weed to grow. Snapping-alert black-brown eyes willed the bread to raise. Every day was molded to her design. Her steps were quick, sure, and sharp as she darted from chore to chore. Had the stiff-beaked bonnet she always wore been aerodynamically correct, her feet would have left the ground.

Tenderness was a weakness she rebuked — if tenderness was a virtue, she was determined to forego the pleasure. Life was tough and she was equal to it. Yet she was the first to appear at the doorstep of a bereaved neighbor or sit at the bedside of a fevered child. The sick, the hungry, the sorrowful sought her guidance and support. She sympathized, wept with them, and goaded them into getting on with their lives.

Tenderness she denied, but it flowed from her every action.

All of her was always in motion. Somehow you never thought of Grandma Suzie as small; every movement was broad and planned. Her gowns—you couldn't call them dresses—covered her from neck to toe, and regardless of the weather, were always long-sleeved. Looking at her you were aware of a slim waist and a full bosom, both of which she effectively concealed beneath voluminous folds of outerwear and several petticoats, topped off with a bib apron.

Whatever came her way Grandma Suzie could handle. She never complained; it was never too hot, too cold, too dry, or too wet.

"What God gives, we take and use" was her creed, the one she had lived by for ninety-five years, and no one had the courage to defy her.

Grandma Suzie was always herself. She never tried to impress other people with up-to-date styles: she wore a bonnet when others were wearing fancy hats, and she wore black, browns, and blues while others wore light colors. She had great strength of character; she did what seemed right, and didn't see the need to conform to anybody else. She didn't let her peers lead her; instead, she led everybody else.

Della Tyrrell ✒ *Sun City Center, Florida*

A lesson on being a good friend...

A Party to Remember

When I was in the fourth grade, I really wanted to be part of the "in" group, but I wore thick glasses, and everyone called me "teacher's pet." I was a very good student, but that didn't seem as important at the time as being popular. Neesha and Diane were the two most popular kids in our town of six hundred people; they were both very pretty, and I wanted to be like them.

My dad had promised to take a group of my friends up to our cabin in the mountains for my birthday party. I decided to invite Neesha and Diane and all the popular boys and girls, but I refused to invite Dorothy Rae and Judy — they were poor, they didn't wear nice clothes, and I didn't want them to spoil things. I guess I wanted to look good in the eyes of the other kids.

"It's your party," Momma said. "But I think you should invite them. You'll be sorry if you don't." Despite Momma's advice, I decided not to.

The day of the party finally arrived and we went around in my dad's blue truck, gathering all the kids. As we went up the hill to pick up a boy named Marvin, I saw Dorothy Rae and Judy standing outside a brown frame house. As we passed them, bouncing our way up the hill on the dirt road, they waved, and everyone waved back. My stomach felt sick, seeing those two girls being left behind in the dust. I felt so bad that I hadn't invited them. That was the worst birthday party I ever had.

I know we traveled up the mountain to our cabin, but I hated the party so much I scarcely remember what we did. I'm sure we ate and hiked around; we must have had a birthday cake, and roasted marshmallows around a campfire. Somebody must have had a good time, but I didn't. All that I could think of was those two forlorn girls standing outside the brown frame house.

The one good thing that came out of that birthday party was that I promised myself that I would never do anything like that again. It was a hard lesson to learn. From that time on, I decided that I would look for people like Dorothy Rae and Judy, who needed friends — that's where I would find my friendships.

Sharie Green ⌐ Arcadia, California

Shooting the Rapids

My son, David, was very active in Boy Scouts when he was growing up. One summer his troop took a canoe trip down the Snake River, in Idaho. I'm sure he'll never forget that experience and the powerful lesson about prayer that it taught him.

On the second day of the trip, they were caught in a swift current when they hit white-water rapids. It was so rough that several canoes turned over. In the banging around, the scoutmaster and guides were having a difficult time righting the canoes and getting stabilized. Then my son noticed one little kid over on the far side of the river. He had overturned and was trying to grab onto a rock, but the rushing water took him over a waterfall. When David looked down, he saw that the boy was struggling to resurface, so he quickly left his canoe and worked his way down the falls to try and assist him. Before he could reach him, the struggling boy's lifejacket brought him to the surface and he was able to make his way safely to the bank.

Just at that moment, a strong current grabbed David and dashed him back into another current and under the falls. He was being smashed onto sharp rocks over and over, until one big rock ripped his lifejacket off. As my son struggled to reach the surface, the water from the falls kept pushing him back under, and he began to get desperate as his air ran out. David made another try to reach the surface, and still another,

until his breath was gone and things started going black. He was scared, really scared, and thought it was the end for sure, until somehow he heard my voice, telling him:

"When you have done all that you can do, ask the Lord and He will take over."

My son desperately prayed with the little strength he had left, and just as he was losing consciousness, he felt a knot slip into his hand. He grabbed it tightly and immediately surfaced to find it was the rope from his canoe, which had worked itself over the falls. As David climbed into the canoe, he realized that the others had been so busy trying to solve their own problems that they had not even missed him. In his time of desperate need the Lord had been his only friend.

There is great power in prayer, and when we rely on it, miracles often occur. Even when we think all is lost and no one can help us, God can and will help if we will only ask.

Sally Neilson — Sierra Madre, California

Pearl Harbor Bride

he Navy is sure shooting close today," my husband sleepily remarked. That morning we had been awakened by loud booming noises. My husband, Elvin, had entered active duty in the Army the day after we were married. Now we were stationed in exotic Hawaii; it was almost like a honeymoon.

The field phone rang, and Elvin quickly jumped up to answer it.

"Get down here quick, Sir," shouted the soldier on the other end of the phone. "The Japanese are bombing the h— out of us." That was how we learned that Japan had attacked Pearl Harbor. In just two hours, more than 4,500 Americans were killed, wounded, or declared missing.

My husband rushed off to his command while I was evacuated to a cavern inside Diamond Head, an extinct volcano. It was a very long day; we had no food and we were so frightened, not knowing what to expect. Late that night some soldiers brought a cardboard box with food—it wasn't very fancy, just thick slices of GI bread with hunks of bologna in between. I worried constantly how my husband was doing. After three long days, a soldier came and took me through the blackout to talk to Elvin on an Army field phone. I was so glad just to hear his voice and know he was okay.

I stayed in that volcano for most of three weeks. Being pregnant, I was sent back to the mainland with the first convoy of servicemen's wives and children, that left the day after Christmas. Elvin came to see me off at the ship and I didn't know if I would ever see him again. I could tell that his heart was breaking and so was mine.

The trip back was arduous. It took twelve days because we were zigzagging back and forth to avoid any enemy submarines that might be chasing us. I went back to live with my parents and there our baby girl was born. Elvin would not see Stephanie until she was almost three years old.

It was a time of unity in my town and in our nation. Everyone was making sacrifices; everybody had someone in the war or was going without. We went through each other's challenges together, not knowing what the morrow would bring. We shared the agony of waiting as our loved ones moved into combat or completed bombing raids over enemy territory. Often you would see a banner in the window of a house as a heart-breaking reminder that a family member had been killed. There would be a gold star for each family member that had been lost. Sadly, some banners had two or three stars.

Everyone pitched in and worked hard. Many left home to work in the shipyards or airplane factories. Most of the doctors and nurses were called into the service, so many of us trained as nurse's aides, to help keep our hospital running throughout the war. Everything was rationed: gasoline, tires, sugar, butter, and meat. We planted victory gardens, and saved everything: newspapers, tin, toothpaste tubes, nylons, and even costume jewelry for the GIs to take to natives when they went to the islands.

After more than three years, I received word that my soldier husband—by then he was a Lieutenant Colonel—was coming home from the South Pacific. When I went to meet him at the train station, it seemed that the whole train was full of men from his command. When they saw our reunion, they shouted, "Kiss her, Colonel!"

When people work together they can accomplish any-thing. Admiral Isoroku Yamamoto, who planned the Pearl Harbor attack, reportedly said, "I fear all we have done is to awaken a sleeping giant and fill him with a terrible resolve."* That oneness, that spirit of sacrifice and patriotism that every-one showed, was a fulfillment of what he said. We all worked together and the giant within us awakened.

Elois Wayment — *Arcadia, California*

From the motion picture Tora! Tora! Tora! *by Gordon W. Prange and Ladislas Farago, Twentieth Century Fox, 1970.*

A lesson on being neighborly...

The Wood-Sawing

When I was a child, stories began "Once upon a time...," but mine will start "A long time ago." A long time ago, wood was burned to provide heat for cooking food and warming the house. When autumn came and the leaves started to turn red, gold, and brown, my parents began planning how to keep our home warm over the winter months. It took a lot of wood to last an entire winter, so every autumn we would have a wood-sawing. This is how it worked.

A wood-sawing was a neighborhood affair, neighbor helping neighbor. My father would go into the nearby woods and cut down as many pine trees as he felt we would need through the cold winter months. The trees were tall—maybe twenty-five feet tall—and sixty inches around at the base. Using a very sharp ax, Daddy trimmed off limbs and cleared them away from the trees. Then the party began.

All the neighbors were invited to come on a certain night after the supper hour. Everyone came, bringing their very sharp crosscut saws and lanterns. The lanterns were hung on nearby trees where their light would flicker over the scene. While the men were sawing the felled trees into blocks about eighteen inches long, the wives and children chatted and played, making "pull candy" or taffy. Laughter and goodwill rang out in the autumn night.

From time to time the men would pause for a break. Buckets of water and gourd dippers were placed on nearby stumps so they could rest and have a cold drink. With everyone working together, one night of cutting provided a family with enough wood for the whole winter. The cut blocks were stacked by the woodshed where my father could split them to use in the iron cookstove or in the tin heater.

At bedtime, the men returned to the house and plans were made for the next wood-sawing. We looked forward to helping another family put up their wood for the winter.

Those days were long ago, when I was only a child. Now I am ninety years old, and when I am cold, I just set the thermostat and heat comes in from vents in the wall. Although modern methods are much easier than sawing and splitting pine logs, in other ways they are not as good. When September comes and the leaves turn bright colors, I long for the closeness we used to feel as neighbors helping neighbors, warming each other through and through.

Viola Eaton — Virginia Beach, Virginia

A lesson on finding the good in others...

Chicken Feathers

*M*y husband, Bill, grew up in a Quaker family. He was taught that there is that of God in everyone, and that of truth, and that it was his duty to find those qualities, even when he disagreed with another's opinion or actions. In Bill's family the children were also honored in this way, even when they made mistakes.

One Saturday night when Bill was about seven, his parents were having a party for twenty-five guests beside their pool. The pool was at a distance from the house, so when Bill's mother needed an aspirin, she sent him to get the bottle from a drawer beside her bed. He gladly went, and when he opened the bedside drawer, he noticed a package of matches laying beside the aspirin bottle. Fascinated, Bill struck a match and held it against the lace skirt that circled the bottom of his parents' four-poster cherrywood bed. The flames quickly spread, and Bill hastily crawled around and under the bed, putting out the fire with his hands. When he thought the fire was all out, he quickly ran to the poolhouse to give his mother her aspirin.

"What's that in your hair?" his dad asked, noticing the bits of ash and scorched lace clinging to Bill's head.

"I've been down by the sandbox," Bill replied, "where we were feathering chickens. It must be chicken feathers."

Well, Dad knew that wasn't true — they had no more feathered chickens that day than flown to the moon. He ran to the house and up the stairs to see what had happened; meanwhile Bill ran down the road and into the woods to hide. When Dad opened the bedroom door, the mattress was in flames! He grabbed a fire extinguisher and quickly put out the fire, but when he went to question Bill, the boy was nowhere to be found. Everyone, including the party guests, set out to find him. They walked up and down the road and through the fields in their evening clothes, calling his name.

Just as the sun was setting, Bill gave himself up.

"I'm sorry, Dad," he apologized; in typical Quaker fashion, his father acknowledged the apology but said nothing more. He lifted Bill to his shoulders and carried him home to bed. He knew that his son had learned a lesson, that nothing more needed to be said.

It's so tempting to tell others what they've done wrong, but we don't usually need to—people already know. Problems need to be dealt with directly in order to be resolved, but afterwards it is just as important to focus on the good in people. If you honor the good in people, they will rise to a level beyond your expectations.

Sue Quigg — Richmond, Indiana

An American Prisoner of War

*D*ecember 7th, 1941, is a day that is still very hard for me to digest. On that day, Japan attacked our U.S. Navy at Pearl Harbor, bringing America into World War II. It stands as the date that changed my world and turned it topsy-turvy. I, as a citizen of my country, cannot write about those days any other way than with deep emotion.

At twenty-two years of age, I was head of our Kawasaki family. My two older brothers, Edward and Corky, were married and lived separately from the family. My father was not with us. He was in Oki Island, Japan, on a one-year visa; as heir to his line, he had legal matters to take care of. Unfortunately, when his visa ran out, Japan and the United States were on a war course and no ships could cross the Pacific Ocean. My father lost his visa rights, and he died in war-torn Japan in 1942.

It still seems like a very bad dream. I was sick with fear, mentally and emotionally, in those frantic days. Day after day, frightening news was posted. Because we were Japanese-Americans, we were suspected as being spies. When the final news came that we would be sent to an internment camp, it was the last blow.

We were given a deadline for our removal to a land of nowhere, but we didn't know what to do with our store and all our family belongings. It was total chaos. I still remember our friends coming to say good-bye after we sold our family possessions — many stayed away, for some reason. The total amount from the sale of our store was $800. It was a last-moment sale.

Our family of five — Mama, Frances, Vernie, Sally, and me — was taken to a makeshift shelter under the grandstand at Puyallup Fairgrounds, a cold, damp, concrete hole. The worst part of the experience was my total loss of trust in my government. My government had failed me; America was no longer my home. Who were we? What was I? I had a number: 1132-C.

We were prisoners and were treated accordingly. We were loaded into a military truck, and crowded like animals being taken to a slaughterhouse. The humiliation resulted in the loss of my dignity as a human being—I was ashamed beyond any words that could ever describe these events. The barbed wires seemed to stick into me for a long, long time afterward.

When we left the detention center after the war, the government gave us fifty dollars apiece for relocation. We went to Chicago to live, but once there, nobody would rent us an apartment. Knocking on the door at one apartment manager's office, I asked if there were any vacancies.

"Are you a Jap?" the apartment manager responded.

"Yes," I replied.

"We don't rent to Japs," she said, closing the door.

I stuck my foot in the door to keep it from closing. As the woman reopened the door, I saw a picture of Jesus hanging on the wall behind her.

"Are you a Christian?"

"Yes," she replied.

"Please let us move in for two weeks and if you don't like us, we'll move out."

The manager agreed to give us a chance. In time, she and I became good friends.

A great nation such as ours cannot afford to cause another such tragedy to befall any group of people. As Americans we must protect each other, as individuals and through the court system. We must use the temperance and wisdom of our forebears to assure our individual rights. We must give each other a chance.

Marge Kimura — Cardiff-by-the-Sea, California

The Experiment

My heart beat fast with excitement each summer when a large canvas tent was set up on the vacant lot next to the post office. It meant the Chautauqua had arrived—the biggest event of the year in the small Virginia village where I grew up. In the days before television, Chautauquas were held in towns all across America. Favorite speakers traveled around the country, teaching and entertaining at these gatherings. Each afternoon and evening for a week, we villagers sat enchanted while song, dance, magic, and melodrama unfolded on the stage. The highlight of each day was a lecture profound enough to make us think and learn.

At age twelve, I considered myself an apt scholar and a deep thinker. When the handsome, middle-aged lecturer greeted us one July day, I leaned forward to hear every word.

"Before I begin," he said, "I would like to administer a test." He took out of his pocket a small, amber-colored bottle, removed the stopper, and held it high.

"You are familiar with the pungent smell of vanilla," he continued. "I want to conduct an experiment to see how far that smell can travel." He gave the bottle a little shake. "As soon as you smell vanilla, raise your hand and keep it up." Almost immediately the hands of nearby listeners shot up.

"Excellent!" he cried, giving the bottle another shake and glancing across the audience. "Excellent!" he repeated as hands began rising from every area. I sniffed and sniffed, but

I couldn't smell anything. I felt left out and inferior. At last I was satisfied—I smelled vanilla. I raised my hand jubilantly, happy to cooperate.

"Thank you," he said, lowering the bottle. "Each of you has indeed a remarkable sense of smell. You see, the bottle contains only water." The man poured a stream of clear liquid into a glass and drank it. I was embarrassed—but wiser. The lesson I learned that afternoon has remained with me. Don't be influenced by others to make hasty decisions. Things aren't always what they appear to be: it is important to think for yourself.

Margaret Campbell ⟶ Richmond, Virginia

The Swimming Lesson

When I was young, in the fifth grade I think, I took my first swimming lesson. Once a week, we walked down to the Elks Club where a big truck waited to take us to Lake Kampeska, about seven miles from town. At first, learning to swim was very scary, but I learned how important it can be to overcome your fears.

The first day we arrived at the lake, I rushed in excitement to a bathhouse to change into my swimsuit. But when I hit that icy water, I wasn't sure I really wanted to learn to swim after all. Lake Kampeska is fed by underground springs, and it's icy-cold all year round. Not only that, but I was afraid. I couldn't see the bottom of the lake, and I was terrified that an awful-looking bullhead fish would come and bite me.

Each of us had to put our faces in the water and blow bubbles, then float on our stomachs and flutter-kick. I soon mastered those skills, and then it was time for the real thing. We climbed onto a large, floating platform and the counselors rowed us out into the lake for a swimming test.

"Gee whiz," I thought, shivering. "We're going out to the middle of the biggest lake in the prairie states—they've never even found the bottom in some places."

Finally the counselors stopped rowing and told us to jump over the side of the platform and dog-paddle, kick, or float anyway we could to get to the pier. The pier looked a long way away.

"I really don't care if all of you want to be first," I told the other kids. "I'll just be last this time." I was trying to sound nonchalant, but the truth is I was just too scared to go first.

One by one, the others made it to the pier despite a lot of coughing, choking, and sputtering, so I decided I had to try. I took a big breath and jumped as far as I could, flutter-kicking and blowing bubbles for all I was worth. I swallowed an awful lot of the lake that day before I found the pier. I was too scared to open my eyes and look for it, so I actually went around the side of it before a counselor grabbed my suit and pulled me up out of the water. My heart had been beating so loudly that I hadn't even heard them yelling at me. Wonder of wonders, I passed my swimming test!

"Oh, it's so easy — anybody can do it!" I told my younger sister.

Once I got over my fear of the water, we had a lot of fun swimming in the lake and I became a strong swimmer and floater. Then one day while I was out swimming, my little brother Harold Gene came to watch. At two years old, he didn't know how to swim yet, so he sat at the end of the dock and dangled his feet over the edge. When Harold Gene saw Mom and Dad coming to join us, he became so excited that he fell into the water. I didn't even stop to think. I quickly swam over to where I'd seen him last, reached down, and yanked him out.

Mom and Dad came running — they were so relieved to find that Harold Gene was okay. I learned a valuable lesson on overcoming fear that day. I was able to pull my little brother out of the water because I was no longer afraid of it. If I had been afraid, there was no way I could have saved his life.

Ruth Brager — *Glendale, California*

Fit for a King

After I graduated from high school, I wanted to go to a college where I could ski and learn to speak foreign languages. My father was a professor at Boston University, and he wanted to make certain I got a good education. We decided upon a college in Switzerland, so at eighteen years old, I sailed off on the Queen Mary bound for Europe.

When I arrived in Gstaad, a picturesque little village in the Alps, it was more exciting than I ever expected. Gstaad was a wonderful little resort with many people coming and going and lots of activity. Several famous people — Rita Hayworth, the Aga Khan, David Niven, Richard Burton, and Elizabeth Taylor — had homes nearby. The ski resort even had a helicopter to carry people up the slopes to ski. When you skied down a mountain in Switzerland, you knew you had skied.

At school, I met all kinds of young ladies from all over the world, from South Africa, Rhodesia, Israel, Mexico, India, Japan, and Australia. Many were daughters of diplomats and other high-ranking government officials in their native countries. Several princesses, including Margaret of Denmark, attended the college.

Although I was young and not used to the wealth and elegance that I saw there every day, I never felt awkward or embarrassed. I had come from a family where etiquette was very important, and I had been taught well. I remember my grandmother sitting in her chair with Emily Post's *Book of Manners* on one knee and *Webster's Dictionary* on the other. Grandmother read Emily Post like it was a novel, and whenever she heard a word she didn't know she looked it up in the dictionary. Grandmother had not had opportunities for much schooling as a child, but she did her very best to learn continually on her own. My mother set her table with a white linen tablecloth and a complete table setting of silver for every meal. She was a real lady; fortunately, she taught me to be one also.

My first year in Switzerland, I was invited to a Christmas dance at the nearby resort hotel. I wore an emerald-green brocade dress, white gloves, and my grandmother's crystal necklace and earrings. Van Johnson, a very tall and handsome movie star, asked each of the girls at my table to dance, but even more exciting than dancing with him was dancing with the King of Jordan.

"Where are you from?" the king asked, in his charming way.

"Have you ever been to Jordan? If you come to Jordan, feel free to reintroduce yourself to me," he graciously offered. We waltzed together the next three dances.

It doesn't matter whether you are in the poorest company or if you are at the queen's table: if you have good manners and they come naturally to you, you will feel comfortable.

Judith Wetherbee Peterson — *Acton, Massachusetts*

A lesson on consequences...

The Dandelion Greens

When I was a little girl, Grandma was my best friend. We had wonderful talks while we dug up dandelions. Grandma loved to cook and eat their leaves, for she believed they were full of good nutrition. I hated the taste of dandelion greens, but I loved the story she would tell while we dug them out of our front yard.

"Do you know how dandelions came west of the Mississippi?" she would ask.

This is how the story went: Grandma's mother, Frances Perry, had left her home in New York one spring to visit her sister on the frontier. While she was there, Frances fell in love with young David Green, who had been recently discharged from the Union Army—he had been the youngest Union soldier to carry a musket in the Civil War.

The couple soon married and moved to the Dakota Territory to homestead, and Great-Grandma Green never returned to New York. She loved her new home, but she was so homesick for the bright yellow dandelions she loved, that she asked her mother to send her some seeds. Well, Grandma Green planted them, and we all know what happened! After dandelions have bloomed, they form fluffy seedpods that can be carried in the wind for miles. Now there are dandelions everywhere, from California to New York. Though bright and sunny, dandelions have been the pest of gardeners ever since.

Grandma told me this story over and over again, and I never tired of hearing it. Whenever I see yellow dandelions, I remember Great-Grandma Green—little did she know what would happen when she planted those tiny little seeds! Her story reminds me to be careful what I do and say. You just never know what—good or bad—may eventually come from the smallest action.

Illa Peterson ⬟ *Clayton, California*

A lesson on making a difference...

Special Delivery

I'll never forget the day Japan bombed Pearl Harbor. My dad had sent me down to the store to get some bread and bologna for supper. While I was there I heard people talking about "being bombed" and about "the war." I didn't hear all they said; they were just standing around talking like folks do in a small grocery store.

I left to go home, but I hadn't gotten far when there was a big explosion. Three huge balls of fire went up. We lived in a railroad town with a lot of gas storage tanks and apparently one had exploded, but I didn't know that—I figured we had been invaded. I ran all the way home, terrified.

During the war, there were plenty of ways for everyone to help. A lot of boys were off in the service, some of them leaving older parents, and I used to chop wood for them—sometimes they would give me an orange or a cookie. One elderly couple I helped, the Beards, had two boys over in Germany.

I also worked for the post office. They gave me fifteen cents to deliver V-mail and special delivery letters. One day I was sent with a special delivery letter to the Beards, with the news that one of their sons was missing in action. The mother almost fell apart. I felt so bad for her. I don't remember the boy's name—I'm old now—but he was like a big brother to me. I was so happy later on when I was able to bring them the special delivery letter telling them that he was okay.

I have a deep-seated love for my country. During those times I learned how important it is to help each other. Even though I was just a young girl, I learned I could make a difference in people's lives. I've always had the notion that if you do something for others, you get it back twofold.

Florence Starry — Idabel, Oklahoma

The Top

*G*o ahead and take it home with you."

I hesitated. Mama and Dad had warned me never to take a toy from a friend at school, in case I later be accused of stealing it from her. But the top my dear friend had brought was most fascinating. I couldn't whirl it like she could, so she urged me to take it home and practice.

I was about eight years old and in the third grade at Missouri Avenue School in Roswell, New Mexico. It was springtime, bringing kites for boys, jacks for girls, and tops for anyone who could flip them just right to spin. These toys occupied us during recess.

When I brought the top home I knew it was wrong, but I just couldn't live without it. I figured Mama and Dad would never get me one of my own. Dad was a teacher on a small income and he spent nothing foolishly. He had lost all his savings in two bank failures during the Great Depression.

Well, I thought of a plan to keep the top. Each afternoon when Dad came home from the school, he chopped kindling wood in one corner of the chicken yard. I got home first and ran out to the chicken yard. There I dug a small hole and buried the top in the soft loam near the woodpile.

When Dad came out to chop kindling, I went out to the woodpile with him. I was playing around here and there, digging roadways for my trike, when I just happened to dig up a top! Would you believe it? When I showed it to Dad as my find of the week, to my dismay he didn't believe my story at all. He put his hand ax down and we sat together on his chopping block. In his usual straightforward manner, he told me that he knew—to this day I wonder how—that I had buried the top and that it was not my property. I confessed that the top belonged to my friend at school.

"Mama and I are disappointed in you," Dad lovingly told me. This broke my heart, and I listened through my tears as he continued. "You broke the rule about taking gifts from friends at school and you acted out a falsehood." I promised him I would always be honest and that I would return the top to its owner the next day.

The very next afternoon when Dad came home from school, he took me to town in our Ford Model T. We went into Woolworth's, where from a counter of hundreds of wooden tops, I got to choose one. Dad drilled holes in its sides to make it hum while it spun. Then he patiently taught me how to wrap the string just right from top to bottom to top again. He also taught me how to throw it to the ground, jerking the string away at the precise instant to make it spin and spin. That day my heart hummed right along with my top, because I knew I was honest.

That top has whirred for many a spin. I still like to try my skill at it, even though I'm seventy-five. There's another reason I've kept that treasured toy all these years: it reminds me of that day when I learned a valuable lesson on honesty.

Catherine Pelsor — *Edmond, Oklahoma*

You'll Find What You're Looking For

I married a man who loves airplanes! After we graduated from college, he joined the Navy and became a fighter pilot, flying jets off aircraft carriers. Fourteen years later, he was selected to command a squadron aboard the USS *Midway*, an aircraft carrier based in Yokosuka, Japan.

We gave our dog to Grandpa and crated up our belongings so that they could be shipped by boat, which would take six months. With our four sons we flew across the United States and across the Pacific Ocean to establish our new home in Japan.

Everyone else had left their homes and relatives back in the States, too, and our squadron-mates became our family for two-and-a-half years. Since I was the commanding officer's wife, I greeted all the new officers and their families and did my best to make them feel welcome. I left a thermos of hot chocolate and a loaf of homebaked yeast bread in their rooms at the Navy Lodge when they arrived. After allowing them time to conquer jet lag, I would call on the wives the next day.

When I met these newly arrived families, I could count on one of two reactions to their coming stay in Japan. The first group moaned about the ordeal of living in a foreign country and had come kicking and screaming with regret. The second group was excited about the adventure ahead of them and the opportunity to see another part of the world and meet new people.

Interestingly, each found exactly what they expected. The pessimistic moaners sat at home and never got involved. The optimistic travelers took trips to Hong Kong, Singapore, Korea, and did some serious shopping. They saw the treasures of Japan, attended Kabuki shows and tea ceremonies, and rode trains to all corners of the islands. They taught English to Japanese ladies and businessmen anxious to improve their pronunciation.

In the process, they made friendships that will last a lifetime. As I rode the commuter trains with my blond, six-month-old son in my arms, I sat beside Japanese mothers with their beautiful, black-haired babies strapped on their backs. Despite our differences, we learned much from each other.

We are allotted only one lifetime. As each moment ticks by, it is gone. What a shame it is to waste those precious moments being negative and unpleasant! How joyful to look for the best in all that comes our way, for I have discovered we find exactly what we are looking for.

Jan Flower — *Tulsa, Oklahoma*

A lesson on appreciation . . .

You Can't Buy Love

ack in the thirties, we lived in Arkansas in what was called the bottomlands, rich farming land that used to be part of the river bottom. My daddy was a farmer and a commercial fisherman. We had eleven children in our two-bedroom house, so Mother and Daddy slept in the living room. Since we had no electricity we used a wood stove — it looked to me like a hog because it was huge and had four legs on it. When it snowed, the snow would blow in through the holes in the tin roof and pepper our faces. I used to think we were poor, but we had a lot more than I ever thought we had.

Every year in the early spring, we had to move out of the house and scaffold the furniture up because the river would flood, and water would come right up into the house. We'd take the chickens and the livestock and go live in tents, hoping and praying that the water would get back down so we could get our crops in. I remember going back home every year and having to scrub and scrub to get out all that black mud. Then we'd move back in.

During the spring and summer, Daddy lived down on the Bay Ditch, the river where he fished. Daddy had nets he would put into the river and he'd catch great big fish, buffalo fish and catfish. Back then there was not a lot of money to be made, but what with fishing and the farming, we made a living. On the weekend we'd get in a boat and go down to see him.

We didn't have any truck or car, so to get places we either had to walk or go in a boat.

My mother made us our own little cotton sacks when we were three so we could pick cotton. When we picked cotton, my daddy would pay us so much according to what we had picked. Mother had poor health, so she'd stay home and cook the meals while we worked. That's a memory! I couldn't wait for that cowbell to ring because I knew it was time to come eat.

At the end of the crop season, I can remember getting out the Sears Roebuck catalogue. We would all sit down together while Mother made out an order for the winter. We lived a long ways from a real store, so Daddy would go to Memphis once a year to buy staples we couldn't get from the Sears catalogue, things like flour, coffee, and sugar. He traveled by train and had his purchases shipped home. It was cheaper than buying supplies in Birdeye, the nearest town. Birdeye was very small; it only had a schoolhouse, a cotton gin, a post office, and a dry-goods store.

I figured the people who lived uptown in Birdeye were high class because they often wore store-bought clothes. My mother made all my dresses, and I thought that was terrible. Also, we had to take biscuits and ham to school while the other kids from town would bring peanut butter and crackers, bananas, or other things they could get from the dry-goods store. Yet, when Mother made us fried chocolate pies for our dinners at school, all the kids who lived in town would fight us for those pies, because they never had anything like that. They were just amazed because we had biscuits and gravy, fried meat for breakfast, and other things they didn't have.

I didn't realize at the time how they envied us; all the time I thought we had nothing and they had a lot. I was ashamed of what we had. I learned when I left home how much we did have and how thankful we should have been. We had everything we needed: hogs and chickens, milk and butter, and more importantly, although we didn't have much money, we had plenty of love. There's a lot of love in a big family. To me that's more important than money or anything else, because you can't buy love. We just had a wonderful life.

Eunice Stout — *Byhalia, Mississippi.*

Zina Taylor Knight

When my grandmother began her fifth pregnancy in 1920, she sensed it would not be a typical case. She was a petite woman, and the pregnancy was difficult and uncomfortable. Grandmother spent a great deal of time on the floor, lying on her side. The doctor confirmed her suspicions with the news that she was carrying more than one baby.

When it was time for the babies to be born, the doctor came to her home in the country for the delivery. Even he was astonished as the babies began to arrive. First came Kenneth, then Kenton. He was followed by Kathryn, and Keith was the last.

In his great excitement to get the story to the newspapers, the doctor left the mother and babies and hurriedly drove the eighteen miles back to town. That night after the doctor left, the lives of Kenton and Keith slipped quietly away. The family was grief-stricken as they worked to save the two remaining babies. Despite their diligence, Kenneth also passed away two weeks later. Now all of Grandmother's efforts went into keeping her precious little girl alive, but without the miracles of science we have today, it was not enough. At twenty days old, little Kathryn died in her mother's arms.

As news of the quadruplet birth spread, Grandmother received letters and gifts from strangers all over the world. One day she pulled them all out of a drawer to show me.

It was always with happiness and a deep sense of joy that Grandmother told me the story of the brief lives and deaths of her babies.

"When the time comes for me to die," Grandmother requested, "do not mourn for me. Celebrate the good news that I've gone to be with my babies." She knew that those four precious infants would be waiting for her in Heaven. She never wavered in that faith.

— *Anonymous*

Caring More

"Don't know. Care less," I said, sarcastically, whenever people asked about my younger brother and sister. That usually put an end to the conversation, and I could get away without revealing my true feelings. People thought I was a pretty horrible little girl. They had no idea the unbelievable hurt and loss I was feeling.

I was nine and the oldest of four children when my mother passed away. Mother was pregnant, but we were very poor and she couldn't afford proper food or medical care. Often when we sat down to eat she went without. I didn't know why then, but I realize now it was because there wasn't enough food. Six months into her pregnancy, she died from a kidney disorder. I was crushed by her death.

Just a few weeks later, we received another blow. My father couldn't deal with my mother's death, so he left town and went away without a word. One summer day, my uncle came over and said we would be staying with him.

We stayed with that aunt and uncle only a short time; they were newly married, and they just didn't have enough room or money to deal with four children. We were sent to another aunt's house in Hershey, Nebraska, a small farming community of 300 people. It was a very challenging time for me: I had lost my mother, my father, and all my friends, and everything was new and different. We had been moved and moved again until it seemed as though nobody wanted us.

Although we were very grateful that our aunt and uncle had taken us in, it was hard to live with them. While she had severe health problems and often had to go to the hospital for several days at a time, he was very harsh and difficult to be around. Yet there we were with no place else to go.

Eventually, my middle brother and sister were sent away to stay with another relative, while I remained and became responsible for my youngest brother, who was two and a half years old. I missed my brother and sister terribly. I felt like my whole family was crumbling, and everything that was dear to me was being taken away one at a time.

So when people would ask me very kindly how my brother and sister were doing, I felt like falling apart and crying and crying. In order to keep from revealing my feelings, I would say in my most flippant, nasty way, "Don't know. Care less."

At long last my father found a new job in another town and our family came together again, but the memory of the pain has stayed with me. We should never judge people from the outside appearances, because we don't really know what is going on inside. Instead, I try to make a person's day better by saying something to help him or her believe in themselves. As a lonely little girl, if I had received love instead of criticism, it would have helped to ease some of the pain.

Jean Moore — Carlsbad, California

Whatever You Are, Be True

On the day I was born, my father presented a diamond ring to my mother. That cold January day in 1915, Dad visited her at the hospital and gave her a beautiful platinum ring with thirty-three diamonds. I am eighty-one years old, and now I wear that diamond ring. It reminds me of my mother. She had many ups and downs in her life, but she never faltered and never complained. I can still hear her say:

"Whatever you are be that; Whatever you say be true."

When I was a little girl, our family was very wealthy. I remember going to the ballpark with my mother to see the Chicago Cubs play baseball. Our family owned the Cubs back then; my uncle Charles Weeghman (who had a large chain of restaurants in the Chicago area) had bought the team and built what today is Wrigley Field. In those days it was called Weeghman Park. On afternoons when there was a game, you'd always see a bear cub in a tall cage outside the stadium. That was the team's mascot.

It was fun to be the daughter of a wealthy family. Mother had a chauffeur and I had a nurse girl and we enjoyed a very nice lifestyle. Unfortunately, it didn't last. My parents unwisely borrowed lots of money to invest in the stock market. The stock market was doing very well, and many people were borrowing money to try to make more money. But when the stock market crashed in 1929 and our stocks became worthless, my parents still had to pay back all the money they had borrowed. We lost everything. We had to go live with my grandmother so that we could survive while my dad found a job. Since the restaurants were gone, he took any kind of job he could get.

Mother had fantastic jewels that meant a lot to her. Those jewels made it possible for us to live. Every month or so we would have to go to the pawnbroker and pawn a piece of her jewelry, a necklace or a ring.

Although Mother never complained, she made up her mind that before she died she would somehow get those rings and pins and bracelets and everything back. It wasn't so much their costliness that mattered to her as it was their sentimental value; she wanted me to have them. Mother worked for a company that made envelopes for years until, bit by bit, she succeeded in reclaiming all of her jewelry.

Through all those harsh experiences, I never heard my mother complain. She had gone so quickly from having great wealth to living in real poverty, but it never depressed her. She knew that who you are is more important than what you possess. This was her motto:

"Whatever you are, be that; Whatever you say, be true."

Dessolyn Weeghman Simmons — *Fort Myers, Florida*

My Dog Spotty

My Aunt Leta had a little fox terrier. When I was about five years old, the dog gave birth to two puppies and I fell in love with a little white one that had brown spots. I wanted him badly, but all of my cousins wanted a puppy, too. I knew Uncle Ned and Aunt Leta would have a hard time deciding who would get the puppies. Then one day, Uncle Ned walked down to our house.

"Shirley, come with me," he said, taking my hand. "Aunt Leta and I have something for you." When we got to his house, Aunt Leta placed the little brown-and-white dog in my arms.

"He is all yours," she said. I think I've never been happier in my life.

I had never told them that I wanted that little dog because I was too shy to demand or even ask for things. But somehow they knew that that little puppy was very important to me. I named him Spotty.

Spotty became my very best friend and he went with me everywhere. When I was in third grade, he even began to follow me to school. The principal got very angry when there were dogs at school, so I did everything in my power to make Spotty stay home. But no matter how I tried, he just wouldn't stay away. I was so afraid that the school authorities would take him away from me.

Mrs. Clawson, my teacher, solved the problem. She knew how to relate to children; she could see that I was in tears nearly every day, so she just let Spotty come to class with me. Spotty became a regular sight in the classroom, sleeping beside my desk all day. When report cards came out, Mrs. Clawson gave Spotty a report card of his own: A for attendance, B for Conduct, and Fs in all other subjects! When the newspaper heard about Spotty's report card, they printed a story about it.

Mrs. Clawson will always have a special place in my heart. Not only was she gentle and kind, but she knew when to bend a rule to keep from breaking a child. She could have had the dog sent to the pound, or she could have sent me home until I returned without him. Instead, she turned a problem into a happy memory for us all—and she saved a little girl a lot of tears.

Shirley Duffy — *El Paso, Texas*

And This Too Shall Pass Away

*M*other was a remarkable woman. She lived in Chicago during the Great Depression. At the time, banks were failing all over the country and a lot of people were losing their money. My folks owned a pharmacy. They had put their money in four different banks, thinking that if one bank failed, the others would still be solvent. Unfortunately, all four banks failed within a few days of each other. Our family was financially ruined. I can still see Mother putting her arms around Dad and saying, "Don't worry, honey. This too shall pass away."

Six years later, they were back on their feet and doing very well. Suddenly, Dad became quite ill and within two weeks he was gone, leaving my mother and me penniless. Since the mortgage contracts were in his name only, the mortgage companies demanded that their money be repaid immediately. Mother could have paid the mortgage in the allotted time, but she couldn't pay it all at once. As a result, our family lost everything again. Mother said, "This too shall pass away."

When I was fifteen years old, I earned a scholarship to go to pharmacy school in Chicago. By this time, Mother had a bad heart and was unable to work, so we moved to Milwaukee to live with my grandmother. I had the full responsibility of supporting both my mother and myself. As I started my sophomore year in high school, I knew there would be no time or money for college, so I gave up my scholarship and changed my major to secretarial subjects. It seemed we would never get ahead, but Mother merely said, "And this too shall pass away."

After graduating from high school, I became a legal secretary making pretty good money. The future seemed bright and promising. In time, Mother and I were able to move into our own house at $25.00 per month rent. Mother was happy. "I told you things would work out," she said.

As the years have gone by, I have often reflected on Mother's words. At times life is challenging, but I have found strength by reminding myself, "And this too shall pass away." If we remember those words, I guarantee that hard times will pass and better days will follow.

Virginia Schaefer — *Sussex, Wisconsin*

Who Will Be There?

My grandchildren love to come and stay at my house. We have a garden and a tire swing; we have a neat tree fort, and lots of bikes and trikes and Big Wheels on the patio. But what my grandchildren really enjoy is that our house is always full of surprises: Who will be there?

About twenty years ago, my husband and I became foster parents. We take care of children whose own parents cannot. Some have stayed just overnight and some have stayed years, so when our grandchildren come to visit there are always other little kids to do fun things with, like play ball or ride bikes.

I began doing foster care so I could give back the love that others have shown me. When I was seven years old, I lived in the Philippines with my family, where my father worked for Del Monte. When World War II broke out between the United States and Japan, my mom and dad and I had to hide in the mountains and jungles because we were Americans. We moved higher and higher in the jungle to avoid the enemy soldiers. Finally, we turned ourselves in at a military hospital, and for three years we were sent from one prison camp to another. I often saw fellow inmates being shot or starved to death.

I was a frightened and hungry little girl in those prisoner-of-war camps, but there were many adults there who were very good to me. Several Catholic priests taught school to me, and another man carried me five miles to a hospital for an operation that saved my life. One couple, my mom and dad's best friends, didn't have any children of their own, so they became my second parents. In those difficult times, many adults helped me through it all.

After my husband and I married, we decided that one day we would help other children through their own hard times. We became foster parents, and since then we have had more than two hundred and fifty foster children. Sometimes the children go back to their own parents and sometimes they are adopted; we are sad when they leave because we love them so much, but we are glad that we can help — that we can give back the love we've been given.

Terry Wadsworth Warne ⏤ *Danville, California*

Grandma's First Job

*D*o you know what responsibility means? Let me tell you what it means and when I learned to be responsible.

Many years ago, when I was just twelve and in the seventh grade, we lived in the country. Our neighbor, Mrs. Dodge, was a schoolteacher. She taught the first, second, and third grades in a schoolhouse that had just one big room. The school was on a hill, close to my house.

Mrs. Dodge needed someone to clean the schoolhouse, to sweep and dust the room, straighten the desks, and even bring in wood for the big woodstove that heated her classroom.

"It will be a big responsibility," she said, "but I know that you can do it. Miss Taylor, the town clerk, will pay you one dollar a week. You will get a check for four dollars at the end of each month." I was so excited that I hadn't even thought about getting paid!

Each day I got up early and went up the hill to the schoolhouse before my schoolbus came. There I started a fire in the stove and brought in wood for the day. After school, I swept, dusted, and straightened twenty-five desks. I had so much fun writing on the blackboard. I pretended I was the teacher and made a drawing for each month, using colored chalk. I made Halloween pumpkins, Thanksgiving turkeys, Christmas angels, Easter bunnies, and lots of spring flowers.

There was also a small pump organ that I sat at and pretended I was playing songs.

In the winter, when the snow was deep, my father would shovel a path to the school for me. He didn't mind; he knew Mrs. Dodge was depending on me, so he gave me lots of support.

I was so excited at the end of four weeks when I went to Miss Taylor's house to get my first check. She wrote my name, then the amount—four dollars—and signed her name. I thought I was the richest kid in the world. For two years I received a check every month, and I had so many things to spend it on.

Many years later, I became a third-grade teacher. But I had no little girl to clean my classroom and draw pictures on the blackboard. I had a custodian instead.

Now, do you know what responsible means? It means that others can count on you to do your job even when it's hard or you don't want to do it. Being responsible makes you feel good. I still remember Mrs. Dodge saying that I was very responsible and that she was so proud of me. I was proud of myself, too.

Stella Brinkley — Eustis, Florida

Laurel Loved Life

Many years ago, Kaye and her family moved into our neighborhood, and she and I quickly became best friends. We pushed our doll buggies together, went to school together, and did all the things that little girls like to do. My mother also became very good friends with Kaye's mother, whose name was Laurel.

Then, the summer after our second grade in school, a polio epidemic broke out throughout the country that would drastically change our lives. For the most part we took the advice of doctors, staying away from crowds and avoiding public swimming pools, but one very hot summer day, Laurel took us to the neighborhood pool. By the end of that day I was showing all the symptoms of polio, and the next day my arm was completely paralyzed. Laurel was devastated. She felt responsible because she had taken me to the pool. She insisted on visiting with me before I was taken to the hospital.

A few days after I arrived at General Hospital in Los Angeles, I was informed that Laurel was also being admitted. She too had been stricken with polio, but far more intensely. She was completely paralyzed from her neck down and she had to be put into an iron lung machine so that she could breathe.

I was very lucky in my recovery, and after eight weeks I was on my way home with only the loss of the use of my right arm. However, it was several years before Laurel could come home. Because of the effects of the polio, she could not move from the neck down, or breathe without the iron lung. Kaye and I visited Laurel weekly while she was hospitalized.

Laurel was sad for only one day. "I wept for one whole day," she said, "but after that I just decided my life would go on."

We were very excited when Laurel came home. Although she was paralyzed, she was mentally whole and we never consider her handicapped. She was our best friend. During the day, Kaye and I took pictures of every corner and place we went so that we could show everything to her. We could hardly wait to run home to tell Laurel every event of our day. She had time to listen and was so very interested.

Laurel is in the *Guinness Book of World Records* for having lived the longest in an iron lung. She spent more than forty years of her life in a four-foot by seven-foot steel capsule. Unable to move from the neck down, she lived life from the neck up where life matters most. She ran her house and raised her family, planned the meals and household schedules, and supervised the daily housecleaning. Her refusal to give in to bitterness and her zest for living kept her going.

Those who knew Laurel and those who will only hear her story will remember her as one who understood the true nature of happiness and of life. This was her gift to us.

Sherry Hombs — Poway, California

Not in My House

When I was twelve years old, good help was hard to find. We lived on a farm in Nebraska along the Platte River during the big drought and the Depression. Circumstances were all very difficult, but my dad was able to hire a man who was a very good worker. Although he handled animals very well, he had such a dirty mouth that it took us by surprise.

One day the hired man spewed out a lingo in the house, and I can remember seeing the shocked look on my mother's face. My dad frowned. "We don't use that language here," he said. The man immediately stopped and apologized. I think he really was sorry and had not meant to speak that way, but his bad language was such a habit that it permeated everything he spoke about.

Apparently there were several other incidents outside, so my father told him:

"I don't care what you say out in the barn, but in my house where my wife and children are, you do not use any profanity."

Well, not more than a day or so later, the fellow was talking—he did like to talk—and again he let go with something. I think the word he said was "d—," which I'm sorry to say I've used. It's not considered a terribly bad word now. Whatever the fellow said, it was just one word, but my dad fired him even though he knew that the hired man would be hard to replace. With my dad, a promise was a promise.

So often nowadays we see and hear terrible things that never would have happened when I was a child. After awhile we can begin to get used to them, but my dad taught me not to tolerate such things. If immorality becomes so common that we are used to it, we begin to accept it by our silence.

Jean Felkins — Poway, California

A lesson on doing your duty...

Grandmother Poulsen

*I*n the town square of Spanish Fork, Utah, you can find a plaque engraved with a picture of a stork carrying a baby. That plaque has my grandmother's name on it, placed there in gratitude for her work as a midwife. Grandmother Anna Poulsen delivered over 2,500 babies in that small farming community.

Anna delivered her first baby when she was only thirteen years old. She had been asked to help a neighbor who was expecting a child. When the time came for the baby to be born, the husband went to get the midwife, but they didn't arrive in time. Anna was not the least bit frightened; she did what the mother told her to do and successfully delivered a healthy baby. She was paid with a piece of calico for a dress.

At the age of twenty, Grandmother took a course in midwifery and soon began working as a real midwife. Within three weeks of her graduation, she had delivered three babies—two boys and one girl. There was no time for her to be idle.

Often my grandmother would come home very weary, having stayed up all night, only to endure a long trip home. One night she was called to a distant town, and by the time she got there in her topless buggy, she was completely buried in snow and so was the horse. After one such trip her feet were so badly frozen that she couldn't wear shoes for six weeks. Early or late, day or night, rain or shine, wind or snow, she would go when called. Babies do not stop to consider the weather when they decide to come.

Everyone came to know who Grandmother Poulsen was. Often little children would stop her on the street and ask: "Where do you keep all your babies? Will you bring me a baby?"

One day while Grandmother was working, her neighbor came running to her. "Mrs. Poulsen! Mrs. Poulsen! Hurry home! Your baby is very sick!" When Grandmother reached home, she discovered that her youngest child had opened the closet door and pried open the chest where medicines were kept. The little girl had poured a bottle of carbolic acid down her chest, and the acid burned her so badly that she died just a few hours later.

On the very day that Grandmother buried her own little daughter, she was called to the bedside of a woman in labor. Despite the terrible pain my grandmother felt from the loss of her own child, she went and delivered a beautiful baby girl. "I was happy for them," she said, "even though my heart was so heavy."

If Grandmother Poulsen were paid in full for all of her services, she would be richer than Rockefeller or Kennedy. Instead she was paid with a dozen eggs, a pound of butter, or sometimes nothing at all. I still have people come to me and exclaim, "Your grandmother delivered my father when he was born!"

Sometimes when I'm bogged down with my own life and I don't feel like helping anyone else, I remember my grandmother's example. She served whenever she was asked, willingly. She often took care of others' needs before her own.

Marva Boyack ⟶ Springville, Utah

Look Me in the Eyes, Jean

In 1937, when I was about four and a half years old, I was allowed to walk to the corner grocery store with Anne, a nine-year-old girl who lived downstairs. We skipped along, laughing and having fun being together. When we got inside the store, Anne went over to the candy display and carefully put a package of gum in her pocket. Then she motioned for me to follow her out of the store.

Outside the store, Anne divided the package of gum in two. I remember thinking that taking the gum was wrong.

"My Dad's going to be very angry with me," I told Anne.

"He'll never know," she said, as we each put two-and-a-half sticks of gum in our mouths.

Sure enough, when I returned home, my father asked me where I got the chewing gum.

"Anne took it and shared it with me," I replied.

"Did she pay for it?"

"No," I answered.

"Look me in the eyes, Jean," Dad said, "and say, 'I didn't do it.'"

I looked at my father and repeated those words without blinking. My father took me by the hand and we went downstairs and got Anne, and the three of us walked back to the grocery store. When we entered the store, the manager approached us.

"One of these little girls took a package of chewing gum," Dad said, "and I came to pay for it." By this time Anne was weeping. My dad paid for the gum and the manager thanked him.

Almost sixty years have passed and I still remember that event as vividly as though it happened yesterday. I have never been tempted to take anything that doesn't belong to me. Above all, I was so proud of my father for being an upstanding man of outstanding integrity. I am always proud to say, "I am Neal's daughter."

Jean Harding Swanson — *Virginia Beach, Virginia*

Santa Don't Know Where I Am

On December 6, 1921, I was the saddest little girl in the whole world. I was riding a train to my new home with my sister, Leota, and my Aunt Lyle. My mother had died fifteen months earlier during childbirth, and my father had died of typhoid fever on Thanksgiving Day. I was left an orphan at nine years old. The seven children in our family were being scattered all over to live with different relatives; one of my brothers was being adopted. Leota and I were going to live with Aunt Lyle, who was a widow and had no children.

It was almost dark when we got off at the station and went to get our suitcases, containing all we owned in the world. As we walked the long six blocks to my aunt's house, a cold wind was blowing. There wasn't much snow on the ground, but the sidewalks were icy and slick. When we arrived at my aunt's two-story frame house, it was very cold because there hadn't been a fire in the house for two weeks — I thought I'd never be warm again. We went to the woodshed for kindling and coal to make a fire. Soon the fire was roaring in the stove, and Aunt Lyle made some hot chocolate that tasted really good.

As time went on, I was still very homesick. Everything was so strange. I'd been put in a lower grade in school than the other children, and I was having a hard time getting acquainted. I had come from being part of a family with seven children to now feeling so alone. I would go to bed at night and pray, and cry myself to sleep in misery, but since I had no other home, I had to learn to live with it.

Finally, it was Christmas Eve. As I was getting in bed that night, Leota asked,

"Aren't you going to hang up your stocking?"

"No, of course I'm not," I answered dejectedly. "Santa Claus don't know where I am now." I really meant it. I felt so lost, I didn't even think Santa would be able to find me.

"Well, then I'll hang it up for you," she said.

"Go ahead. It won't do any good. There won't be anything in it."

When I got up on Christmas morning, I was so surprised. There was a beautiful Christmas tree, all decorated. My family had never had a Christmas tree before! Then I looked in my stocking — there was the most beautiful doll I'd ever seen. The doll was made of porcelain, and it was wearing a pretty pink dress. Its blue eyes opened and shut when I laid it down and picked it up, and it had beautiful, shiny black hair.

That doll meant so much to me, giving me hope at a time when I thought all was lost. I felt that if Santa knew where I was, then God must know, too. With hope, I was able to carry on.

Juanita Cash — *Paso Robles, California*

Mother Was Never Idle

t first, spending six weeks in bed sounded won-derful. I had been diagnosed with hepatitis and was feeling ill and utterly wasted. The doctor ordered complete bed rest. At that time, the oldest of our five children was ten, while our twins were only four years old. They kept me very busy, but with hepatitis all that I wanted to do was sleep.

After the first week in bed, my symptoms improved considerably, and I felt like getting back to my usual routine. Unfortunately, I still needed to stay in bed for five more weeks to protect my liver from being damaged. I could read and talk on the telephone, but I soon learned that having nothing to do was awful.

My mind went back to my childhood and growing up in a small farming community. At the age of three, I had begun helping with chores around the house and yard. I remember sitting on the floor with my legs wrapped around our butter churn, turning the crank. The crank turned pad-dles that churned the cream into butter. I also took scraps to the chickens and pigs. When I was just a little older, I deliv-ered milk to some of our neighbors and earned a penny a quart. I remember pulling a wagon filled with milk bottles.

As I grew up, I helped with many other tasks—dusting, mopping floors on hands and knees, making bread, cooking, and picking and canning berries and other fruits and vegetables. I ironed, fed the animals, and helped Dad with some of his chores. When I was old enough to handle a horse, Dad let me steer old Dolly as he loaded hay on the wagon. Then we would bring the load of hay home from the field to put in the barn.

I enjoyed being old enough and mature enough to assume responsibilities, even though I didn't always like the tasks assigned to me. I remember thinking that when I became an adult I was not going to work as hard as my mother worked.

Mother worked quickly, and I never remember seeing her idle. Whenever she sat down, she peeled apples, mended, or read. Mother told me many stories, usually with some moral lesson attached, but always as she worked. I was convinced that she actually liked to work. Why, I did not know.

My mother was also a newspaper correspondent for the two major newspapers in our state. She covered any news from the three small communities in our mountain valley. When I was a baby, Mother held me, nursed me, and cared for me while writing details for news articles on the painted woodwork near the phone. Later, when I was asleep, she copied the notes onto a piece of paper, wrote the article, and then washed the woodwork.

Today I'm glad I don't have to work as hard physically as my mother did—washing with a wringer washer, hanging clothes on the line in summer or winter, baking and canning with a coal stove, and cleaning the feathers from a chicken before cooking it—but I have learned that work can be satisfying, and that accomplishing a task can have many rewards. It certainly is a blessing to be able to work. From Mother I learned that if you want to do something, you can usually find the time and a way to do it.

Helen Read — *San Diego, California*

Memories Worth Keeping

I grew up in Germany during World War II, when the people and things around me could so quickly be destroyed. As a result of this, I realized that so many things are changeable — health, possessions, friends, where you live, and even life itself. During those terrifying times, I would cling to memories of happier, more carefree days. I decided that when I was a mother and a grandmother, I would make it a point to create memories that would be special to my children and grandchildren. Whatever else you may lose, memories will always be there.

When my children were young we did not have much money, so the memories we made were simple ones that brought much joy. We would walk down to the beach with a carton of milk and some animal cookies as a special treat. My two children and I would pretend the sea foam was really mermaid's milk, and we'd roll up our pantlegs and hop over the foamy edge while drinking the milk we'd brought.

Other times we had a penny walk: We'd explore the neighborhood and at each corner we'd toss a penny to decide whether to turn right or left or to continue straight. We'd have birthday parties complete with cake and party dishes for wooden ducks and various dolls and bears. In later years, when money was more readily available, we went to museums, on bus, train, or tram rides. We went camping — although I'm not fond of it myself — and we traveled abroad to study languages.

Through spending one-on-one time with my children and grandchildren, by listening to their concerns, and by attending their recitals, plays, and class presentations, we have shared many happy times together. I've discovered that while I was giving them memories worth having, I was also building a treasury of memories for myself. Whatever else may happen, those memories will always be there.

— *Anonymous*

The Easter Egg Hunt

"Clickety-clack," "clickety-clack," awakened me, reminding me that I was on a train headed for Washington, D.C. That morning, my brother Russ and I had boarded a commuter train to visit "the Aunts" and our sister, Anne, for Easter.

"The Aunts" were Father's two older sisters: Aunt Grace was little and plump and everyone called her Birdie, while Aunt Ellen, or Kit, was taller and quite thin with a shock of reddish hair. The Aunts went to Washington every winter to get away from the harsh New England weather, and this year they had taken Anne, as she too was sickly.

The Aunts' chauffeur met us at the train station with their limousine, and the days following we spent sightseeing. We saw the cherry trees along the Potomac all in bloom— they looked like huge fluffy clouds with their white petals drifting down like snowflakes, and they smelled oh-so-sweet. We also went to the Washington Monument; it looked like a white marble needle pointing up to the sky.

I liked the Lincoln Memorial best. Lincoln, with his rough but gentle face and those huge hands lying relaxed on the arms of the marble chair— his sadness touched me even as a child of seven. As I walked up the wide white marble steps to the huge bronze statue of Lincoln, his penetrating eyes seemed to look right inside me.

The following Sunday was Easter, and the Aunts had a surprise for us. They had purchased beautiful summer dresses of dotted Swiss for Anne and me. The dresses had little puff sleeves trimmed with lace and Peter Pan collars made of lace — they even had colored bloomers to match! With white knee socks, black patent-leather Mary Jane shoes, and white straw bonnets with ribbons to match our dresses, we were all set. Then, to top it all off, we wore white lace gloves. Oh, how we twisted and turned before the full-length mirror! Boy, weren't we some pumpkins? The Aunts were dressed in calf-length, flowing dresses with big Easter bonnets piled high with flowers and ribbons.

The chauffeur dropped us off at the White House. Imagine, we were inside the fence on the White House lawns! There were dozens and dozens of children of all ages with their parents, but we evidently had a special place as the Aunts and Russ had chairs with their names on them.

Then it was time to line up for the Easter egg hunt. Oh, goodie! Anne said she was too big to hunt eggs with children, and she went and sat with the Aunts. Not me — at seven I was still a kid. We were all given straw baskets with green paper grass in them. I didn't find many eggs, but it was fun watching the real little ones toddle around, and I helped them locate an egg or two. Some children found the gold eggs, the silver eggs, the largest and the smallest ones and they were given little gifts.

Suddenly, there was a kind of a murmur, and the older people stopped talking and the little ones stopped running around. It became very quiet, and I saw a man and woman coming towards us. The man was in a dark suit and he was holding the arm of the lady. He was tall and thin and kind of homely — he reminded me of Abe Lincoln. The lady was tall, almost regal, in a flowing, flowered chiffon dress. She had such a lovely smile. Her black hair was parted in the middle and combed straight back into a bun on the back of her neck.

A large, white picture hat made a frame for her kind face. She reminded me of our mommy. I knew who they were — President and Mrs. Calvin Coolidge.

Even at such a young age, my throat felt tight and I felt tears behind my eyes. Imagine, I was in the presence of the President of these whole United States. I was on the grounds of the White House — me, Olivia Angier Chandler. It was a sensation that I have felt only a few times in my life. It was a sensation like when the flag of the United States passes and men uncover their heads and we all put our hands over our hearts, or when we sing "The Star-Spangled Banner" or "America the Beautiful." I guess that feeling is patriotism.

Olivia Walker Priller — *San Diego, California*

GRANDFATHERS, GRANDMOTHERS, PARENTS, SINGLES: If you have a story you would like to submit for possible use in our future books, please contact:

ALTI Publishing
P.O. Box 28025
San Diego, CA 92198-0025
Fax: (619) 485-9878
e-mail: altipub@ix.netcom.com

Comments also will be welcomed concerning this book or suggestions for future books to benefit children, parents, and families.

ALTI Publishing offers quantity discounts or special edition printings for individuals, corporations, or other groups interested in strengthening traditional values.